The **Centennial**
of a **Great Idea**

Recalling a Lifetime of Experiences
in the National Park Service

Phillip R. Iversen

Printed and bound in the United States of America
First printing • ISBN # 978-0-9908913-7-6
Copyright © 2016 Phillip R. Iversen

TO ORDER ADDITIONAL COPIES OF:

The Centennial
of a Great Idea
Recalling a Lifetime of Experiences
in the National Park Service

by Phillip R. Iversen

CALL: 1-800-628-0212
ALL MAJOR CREDIT CARDS ACCEPTED

SCOTT COMPANY PUBLISHING
P.O. Box 9707
Kalispell, MT 59904
Toll Free: 1-800-628-0212
Fax: 1-406-756-0098

TABLE OF CONTENTS

INTRODUCTION

The year 2016 will be the centennial year of the National Park Service, as an agency of the Federal Government. Several National Parks existed prior to creation of the agency and were managed as stepchildren of various agencies, such as Yellowstone managed by the U.S. Army. Centennials are a span of history, a time of reflection on what has happened, what has changed and where do we go from here. I have lived a long life and this book is my contribution to the historical record.

I spent thirty years, during an interesting period, working for the National Park Service, met some fascinating people and witnessed many events that need to be recorded. I hope that people who love the National Parks will also enjoy this look inside the daily activities of the agency and feel comfort that there are a lot of dedicated employees caring for these national treasures.

My family lived in Eugene, Oregon during the early 1920s and in fact I was born in Eugene. While living in Oregon, the family visited the local National Park areas of Crater Lake, Yosemite and Oregon Caves, so I was aware of National Parks but as a child had only a vague idea of their purpose. It is possible that the photos in our family albums and family conversations about these visits had left an imprint on my subconscious mind and made me receptive to the experiences I am about to relate. However, at this time like many people, I assumed that National Parks were a part of the U.S. Forest Service rather than a bureau of the U. S. Department of the Interior. I think this misunderstanding is partly due to the image of Smokey Bear, a U. S. Forest Service icon - but Smokey is wearing a National Park Ranger hat? I am not aware that Forest Rangers ever wore this style of hat.

I have worked in twelve National Park Service locations including two non-park assignments, as Assistant Regional Director of the Midwest Regional Office in Omaha and as Utah State Director in Salt Lake City. Of the Parks I have worked in, it is interesting how many of them were created largely through the efforts of a single individual rather than a coordinated effort of an organization.

A hundred years ago in this country, transcontinental highways did not exist and the roads that did exist were little more than unimproved trails.

There were very few motels, gas stations and other creature comforts along the way. The gas stations only operated from 8:00 am to 5:00 pm so daily destinations had to be planned accordingly. Consequently, tourism was not a major industry and the value of National Parks had to compete with more practical land uses such as farming, timber and mining. For these reasons, proposed National Parks often received strong opposition in the local communities.

I never worked at Yosemite National Park, but it was a classic case of preservation through the efforts of one individual, John Muir. I did work at Rocky Mountain National Park and Enos Mills had a major roll in the creation of that Park.

I transferred to Canyonlands National Park as Chief Ranger just a few months after it was established. Superintendent Bates Wilson of remote, little-known, neighboring Arches National Monument (now a National Park) was the champion of this now very popular Park. Superintendent Wilson was not the typical spit and polish office manager, but he was a fantastic cowboy, chuck wagon cook/trail guide and storyteller. Bates was one of the most naturally talented public relations people I have ever known.

In 1959, I was assigned to the newly proposed Chesapeake and Ohio Canal National Historic Park Project as the first Park Ranger and part of the total staff of four people, consisting of Superintendent, Office Secretary, Chief of Maintenance and myself. As I recall, the federal government acquired the old canal as part of a tax settlement with the current owner, the B & O Railroad. The old canal follows the very scenic Potomac River for one hundred and eighty miles, and the plan was to obliterate the old canal and build a freeway into Washington, DC. Fortunately, Supreme Court Justice William O. Douglas had been using the old canal tow path as a hiking trail and he fought successfully to save the canal from destruction, which would have been a tragic loss.

So these are just a few examples of how individuals have saved areas for National Parks and now millions of us should be grateful to them for their tenacity and vision. The least we can do is remain vigilant in protection of the Parks for our children and future generations. As John Muir once said, "Anything that has value is vulnerable."

CHAPTER I
ZION NATIONAL PARK
1948 - 1949

The greatest life-changing event of my life occurred in a speech class while attending Dana College in Blair, Nebraska. The purpose of the class was to develop skill in creating and delivering various types of speeches, some planned, some impromptu before an audience, similar to a Toastmasters club. On this particular day, my fellow classmate Art Sorensen gave a speech before the class and related his experiences of the previous summer, as a seasonal Park ranger at Zion National Park in Utah. Art's talk was fascinating in many respects and I was very interested in learning that the National Park Service hired part time employees during the summer months.

Zion National Park, Utah

Mr. Sorensen's talk really fired my interest and after class I questioned him extensively about the federal government employment process. Art had worked the previous two summers at Zion but was pursuing a career as a Lutheran minister, which precluded a return next summer to Zion. Maybe his job would be open. After this conversation I went to the local post office in Blair and obtained a quantity of U. S. Government standard job application forms, filled them out and mailed to all the Parks known to me. Hal Jersild was a good friend and I talked him into joining me in the work application process. In fact, I filled out some of his forms and mailed them together with mine.

We received a couple of possible job offers, but the most encouraging response came from Mr. Fred Fagergren, Chief Ranger at Zion National Park. I had used Art Sorensen as a reference and fortunately he had left a very good impression with Park officials. Mr. Fagergren offered jobs to both Hal and me, enclosing a packet of information about Zion and details of our job description.

Let me pause for just a moment and reflect on this very brief, most likely inconsequential incident. I never cease to be amazed at how this trivial event had such consequences. IT CHANGED MY ENTIRE LIFE – FOREVER! as you will learn shortly. Art Sorensen was a year or two ahead of me in college. He and I were pursuing different careers in college, we just happened to be in this one class together. Had his speech been given at any other time of the year it would not have been significant because the time span in which the National Parks hire summer employees was a brief window early in the calendar year. If Art gave that talk a month later and I was inspired to send a job application, it would have been too late – all summer positions in the National Parks would have been filled.

Back to the story. The first thing Hal Jersild and I had to do in preparation for our new job was purchase the ranger uniform, at our own expense, from Fechheimers Uniform Suppliers. These uniforms at the time cost $125.00, a lot of money for a college student. The uniform was expensive, but the Stetson hat was really expensive and as best I can remember the cost was about $50.00. Remember these are 1948 prices.

The first day on the job, Hal and I were taken on a tour of the facilities by Chief Ranger Fred Fagergren. The ranger dorm was a beautiful, fairly new building and probably the best ranger dorm within the entire National Park System. Some senator, congressman or influential person within the system must have had a soft spot in his heart for Zion. The dorm was also situated in an enchanting location, a natural amphitheater surrounded by the West Temple and Towers of the Virgin, which rose up to an elevation of almost eight thousand feet, about four thousand feet above the floor of Oak Creek canyon.

Towers of the Virgin, Zion N. P.

The maintenance area for vehicle storage and repair shops was built against a cliff wall, across the amphitheater from our dorm. As we approached the maintenance area, the first visual impact was an immense boulder the size of a small house, resting on top of a brand new Dodge pickup truck and a tractor trailer used to transport heavy equipment, such as a bulldozer road grader. Both vehicles were flattened to about two feet in thickness and it required workers more than a week with pneumatic jackhammers and dynamite to remove the rock. This dramatic scene caused me to ponder the hazard of living at the bottom of a canyon.

Ranger Dormitory, Zion N. P.

The location of the ranger dorm was the homestead site of a Mormon family, the Crawfords, and when Zion National Park was established first as a National Monument in 1909, the Crawfords and several other Mormon pioneer families were forced to sell their land to the government and move to a new location outside the new Park boundary. It was fortunate that the children of some of these families now worked for the Park, including J. L. Crawford who eventually became one of my closest friends. J. L. told me that his family farm consisted of seventeen acres, and they owned a cow, chickens and had a large garden. Within this small tract of land the Crawford family was able to provide for their needs and there were several children in the family. Remnants of an old irrigation canal for the farm was still clearly visible at this time and I think it can be located today.

During the first year at Zion, most of my duty consisted of working in the east and south entrance stations to the Park collecting entrance fees from visitors. Each ranger working at the entrance stations had his own cash box and we were issued four books of fifty, numbered entrance permits, each worth one dollar. The permit was good for, as I remember, three days or maybe one week, including campground fee. We were responsible and liable for those tickets and if any were lost we covered the loss at our own expense.

The entrance permits were checked out from the chief clerk, Mr. Fred Novak (the position is now called administrative officer) and when the tickets were sold we transferred the money and ticket stubs from our cash box to a canvas bag, which was locked with a special padlock that recorded a successive number each time it was opened. Forms were filled out to record this number and signed. When the money bag was delivered to Mr. Novak, he also signed the form and gave us a copy, which released us from further responsibility for the entrance tickets and money.

At this point in the history of Zion National Park, visitor travel was light and it might take three or four days to sell four books of entrance permits, or two hundred. In the meantime we kept the cash in our money box with us on duty and under our bed at the dorm each night. Mr. Novak would not permit us to submit coins, only paper money. There was no bank in the small village of Springdale just outside the Park, so no place to exchange coins for paper money. This might not seem to be a big problem, but most visitors entering the south entrance of the Park had traveled through Las Vegas, Nevada, seventy-five miles southwest, where silver dollars were used in the gambling casinos. We always accumulated a lot of silver dollars. We had to get rid of this hard money in making change so the poor visitor that gave us a twenty dollar bill to buy a one dollar Park permit usually received nineteen silver dollars in change.

The Utah Parks Company, manager of the concession operations at Zion, Bryce Canyon and the North Rim of the Grand Canyon, gave a big discount on meals to rangers at the cafeteria and dining room of the lodge, providing we were in uniform. Our presence was a good recommendation of the food and we were available to answer questions from Park visitors. All meals at the cafeteria were discounted to fifty cents. Breakfast at the lodge was also fifty cents, I think lunch was about seventy-five cents and dinner ninety cents for anything on the menu.

Despite the bargain meals at Park concession facilities, we quickly tired of eating the same food each day and we ate most of our meals at the Canyon Inn Café in the neighboring town of Springdale, operated by Danny and Helen Exell. They served excellent food and also grubstaked us by allowing us to charge our food until payday, which was every two weeks. This was important because sometimes paydays were without pay. The reason was the U.S. Congress was usually slow about passing appropriation bills by July 1st, the beginning of a new fiscal year. Contrary to current procedure, until an appropriation bill was passed the government could not issue checks. This situation happened each year on July 1st and sometimes it was two, three or more weeks until we were paid. The good Excells carried us through those times of need and we bonded very closely to them. Years later Danny and Helen built a nice motel on the south edge of Springdale called the Driftwood Lodge. Many years later when I was Utah State Director for the National Park Service and visiting the area, I always rented a room with them, still a loyal customer.

The Switchbacks, Zion N. P.

We did a lot of hiking at Zion on our days off and on one backcountry trip in the Kolob, Hal Jersild and I became lost – well – not really lost because we knew where we were in the bottom of several interconnecting canyons, but we couldn't find the trail out of the place. The Kolob is a remote area west of Zion Canyon, with a primitive road access and a part of what was then Zion National Monument. No Park visitors ever ventured into this undeveloped and backcountry area. The only man-made structure within the entire monument was a rustic fire lookout station in the Kolob called Lava Point.

Chief Ranger Fred Fagergren was driving up to the Kolob for a routine inspection and gave us a ride to Lava Point. Fred dropped us off at the top of Hop Valley trail, gave us very brief directions for our hike and how to locate the exit at the end of our trip to U. S. Hwy 93, south of Cedar City, and we would hitch hike back to the Park. If Fred had hiked this route it was a long time ago because he had forgotten some important details. Hop Valley trail was little more than a game trail, four to five miles in length and at the north end makes a long, steep descent to La Verkin Creek. This was intended to be a one day hike, so Hal and I only carried lunch, no extra clothing, bed roll or tent. Because it was a crude trail and difficult descent, daylight was fading by the time we reached the bottom of the canyon and continued the long journey west down La Verkin Creek.

The canyon was narrow in places and we had to walk in the creek part of the time, or jump back and forth across it. I recall one of those jumps; it was getting dark and I mistook a gob of foam in the creek for a rock. I jumped for this rock and much to my surprise dropped up to my waist in a pool of cold water. The hike down La Verkin Creek was another three or four miles in length. Our directions from Fred were to turn to the right, north, when we reached the confluence of La Verkin Creek and Timber Creek, go to Kolob Canyon and through the "gap" (Taylor Creek) out to U.S. Highway 93. When we reached Timber Creek it was really dark in the bottom of the canyon and we couldn't locate the "gap". Fred said it was only a short distance north to the point where we would exit these canyons, but in fact the distance was more like five miles and then another two or three miles out to Hwy. 93. We now had no idea how to exit from this canyon, but I did know that the big black ridge high above us to the west separated us from U. S. Hwy. 93.

We didn't even have a jacket and it was getting cold. I told Hal, "We don't know where the trail is or which way the trail goes, but I am sure the highway is on the other side of this ridge, so that's the direction I'm going." However, it was too dangerous to climb the steep ridge in the dark, so we huddled together and tried to sleep. We couldn't even build a fire because our matches had gotten wet wading in La Verkin Creek. I don't think either of us slept, just shivered all night and at the first light of dawn we began our struggle up Black Ridge Mountain.

Once reaching the top, sure enough we could see the highway, way off in the distance, but we were confronted with a treacherous descent of Black Ridge in front of us. There were many sheer cliffs that we would not be able to negotiate without a rope, but there were also intermittent talus slopes composed of small, loose, volcanic rock resting at an angle of repose that would slide if disturbed. If we should lose our footing and balance, we would roll and bounce all the way to the bottom of the mountain. The only way to make a safe descent was to put one foot under our butt, extend the other leg in front acting as a brake, hands to either side and hopefully make a controlled slide with the loose rock.

Upon reaching the bottom it was about a mile or two hike to the highway where we planned to hitch hike back to the Park. Fortunately, one of the first vehicles to come along was a Utah Parks company bus returning with railroad passengers from Cedar City and the driver recognized us. The Park staff was aware that we were missing and about to launch a search party, but we were back at the dorm by early morning hours with a happy ending to our adventure. Hal and I were greenhorns and really didn't plan our trip carefully by studying topographic maps, we didn't have proper equipment and supplies. However, at this time in history a lot of hiking was done on well-maintained trails, with virtually no backcountry bush whacking. Modern hiking boots and equipment didn't exist, dehydrated food was not available, I don't recall ever seeing a backpack.

I remember another occasion at Zion when a group of us made a stupid hike in the dark. We were hiking on the west rim trail and on the long, steep descent north of Angels Landing we met a mule deer coming toward us on the trail. The trail was only about three or four feet wide, an almost sheer drop on one side and a steep, solid sandstone rock cliff on the other side. We managed to work into a sitting position and inch our way up the sandstone ledge far enough to allow the deer to pass. Shortly after this delay in our schedule it became so dark we could hardly see the trail in front of us. In fact, we found some walking sticks that we probed in front, like a blind person, to make sure we didn't walk off the edge of the trail, which dropped precipitously for fifteen hundred feet. When you're young you're invincible.

My companions and I hiked most of the trails of Zion but on one occasion we rented horses from the Mormon Bishop of Springdale, our gateway community, and made a memorable trip up Parunuweap Canyon, along the east fork of the Virgin River. This was a remote area and at this time of little hiking, few people had visited there. The first mile or two are on private land and just before entering the Park, there are ruins of an old pioneer homestead called Shunesburg. Mr. Shunesburg was a polygamist and built this beautiful house of quarried sandstone rock, with three or four individual apartments, one for each wife. My college studies at this time were in Architectural Engineering and I was very impressed with the solid, beautiful construction, by one man in a remote location working with simple tools. I later learned that the ranger dormitory of Zion was modeled after this building. There was an old apricot tree growing near the house, loaded with delicious, juicy, golden apricots and we sat on our horses picking the fruit for a refreshing snack.

Shunesburg House, Zion N. P.

Both years working at Zion I worked through the deer season, I think it was late October. My mode of transportation was a 1942, 442 Indian motorcycle. On my return to Illinois I didn't want to cross the Colorado Rockies this late in the year, so headed south on U. S. Hwy. 89 to Flagstaff, Arizona where I would pick up U. S. Hwy. 66 and head east. The weather was not good and as I reached Jacob's Lake, at about 8,000 feet elevation, near the north rim of the Grand Canyon, it started to rain, sleet and snow. I was wearing all the clothes I could pile on but water from the road sprayed up from the front wheel of the motorcycle, soaking my pants and the cold wind was blowing up my coat sleeves. This cold, damp weather persisted all the way through Arizona, New Mexico, Texas and Oklahoma. The colder it got the faster I drove, but with frequent stops for hot chocolate to warm up. I was so wet and cold that it would take several minutes to quit shivering and shaking so violently that I couldn't hold a cup steady without spilling the contents.

At a roadside restaurant in Oklahoma, God certainly intervened to save me from self-destruction. I had stopped at a little roadside diner and was sitting at the food counter, shaking from cold, trying to drink hot chocolate when a truck driver sat down on the stool next to me. He said, "You passed me like a bolt of lightening some distance back and you're going to kill yourself driving that fast on these roads. Why don't you load your motorcycle in the back of my semi trailer and ride with me at least to Oklahoma City." I was thrilled with the offer and he no doubt saved me from injury or worse. Acts of kindness such as this one never forgets.

CHAPTER II
DESTINY DEFIES ALL ODDS
1950 - 1954

After completion of the second long season working as a seasonal Park ranger at Zion, I hitched a ride back to Illinois with Bob Barrel, a seasonal Park naturalist at Zion. Bob's home was Worcester, Massachusetts and he had completed his second year at Harvard University.

Bob owned an ancient DeSoto coupe automobile and the ride home was quite an adventure. We were traveling back east on U.S. Hwy. 6, now Interstate 70, through Colorado. In the late afternoon we had passed through the attractive little city of Glenwood Springs and about at sunset we had just passed the tiny town of Minturn on our way to Vail Pass. Going up a steep grade the old DeSoto made a loud, ominous clunking noise and shuddered to a stop. We managed to push the car backward across the highway and headed downhill, hoping to make it back to the Minturn turnoff.

A good Samaritan heading west stopped to investigate our plight. We asked if he could tow us to a garage in Minturn, but he said there was no garage in Minturn and anyway it was a Saturday night and nothing was open. To make a long story short, he tied a chain to our bumper and towed us the entire seventy miles back to Glenwood Spring. Bob and I had very little cash between us but wanted to pay this kind man for the long haul and saving us from a cold night in the mountains. He wouldn't take payment for helping us and only asked that if we ever had the opportunity to help someone else in distress, that we would also be a good Samaritan. That act of kindness will forever be an inspiration, and I wonder if such a thing could happen today.

It required about a week to repair the transmission of the DeSoto and we resumed our journey east. We had crossed the Continental Divide, reached the prairie of eastern Colorado and as dusk was approaching we could see the town of Brush, Colorado a couple miles ahead. Once again it was late in the day and beginning to get dark. Suddenly the headlights blinked, the engine sputtered and we came to a stop. We were still a couple of miles from town and somehow got the car started again and sputtered on, but the lights still didn't work. Anyway we made it to town, but after business hours. Fortunately, the Ford dealership and some of its large garage doors were open and the building fully lighted. It was a large, good-looking business. The big door to the shop was open, just ready to close when we rolled in. As we walked into the showroom/business area a girl shouted at me, Hey Phil! It turned out to be the daughter of the man who owned the garage and she was a classmate of mine from Dana College. That chance meeting of an acquaintance was another stroke of good fortune, because the garage remained open long enough to fix our car and the cost was just a couple of dollars. Thanks again to another good Samaritan and that guardian angel on my shoulder.

After working an extended season for two years at Zion National Park, attending college at Dana College and Iowa State University, I returned to McNabb, Illinois to pick up my belongings and ponder my next move. My father had recently retired as pastor of the Lutheran church in McNabb and they had moved to Luck, Wisconsin to be near my sister. For a short duration I rented a room in town and ended up working again at the Swain Hatchery until I decided where to go. It turned out to be a longer stay than originally anticipated. I ended up marrying Patricia, the boss's daughter.

About a year later, Patricia's uncle who was my age, joined me in forming a business partnership and we purchased the Henry Produce Company in the neighboring town of Henry, Illinois. We worked hard, working long hours six days a week and had a thriving business, but after making our loan payments, our meager salaries plus one employee, we were going nowhere. I never got over my Park Service experience and the exhilarating satisfaction of living in the west. I was restless, uninspired and dissatisfied with a future career in the produce business and not pleased with the future prospects.

By this time Patricia and I had a little baby boy and the chances of other opportunities were closing in on me – not a happy thought. Despite being the son of a Lutheran pastor, I have an unorthodox concept of God, not an anthropomorphic human image (God created man and man created God) and do not believe a God manages our daily lives. However, my life has been a steady stream of fortunate events that occasionally make me wonder who is my guardian angel? Once again those strange forces worked to bring about another event that changed the direction of my life, in a dramatic and positive way.

A family friend of Patricia's parents, Marguerite Moore (Mrs. Fred Moore) had dedicated her life to raising her grandson, Fred Moore III, who had lost his mother at childbirth. Freddy at this time was about ten years old and suffered from severe asthma attacks in the humid Illinois climate. To mitigate the problem, Marguerite purchased a home in Phoenix, Arizona where she and Freddy spent the winter months. She paid for the cost of this lifestyle by operating a real estate office on the southwest corner of Central Avenue and Coolidge Street, just a short distance south of Camelback Road in Phoenix. She owned a home a few blocks west, at 400 West Coolidge Street.

In August 1953, Marguarite Moore invited Patricia and me to assist her in driving to Phoenix. She was truly an angel, a wonderful, compassionate lady, always ready to go someplace - the horse track, Nogales, Mexico, shopping or just sightseeing around town. She was a delightful and interesting person for people of all ages to be around. Marguarite told me that we could travel by any route we wished, providing we arrived in Phoenix by a certain date because Freddy had to be ready for the new school year. We also had the pleasure of traveling in her big, new Buick Roadmaster car.

The most direct and fastest route from Illinois to Phoenix was the famous Route 66, but we chose the more scenic U.S. Hwy 34 and 40 to Denver and Rocky Mountain National Park. Little did I know that someday I would be working in this Park as a permanent ranger. From there we continued west to Spanish Fork, Utah and the junction with U.S. Hwy 89, then south. We made a quick side trip through Bryce Canyon National Park, then on to Flagstaff, Arizona and Phoenix.

Hold on to your hats, because here again a most amazing event happens that defies all odds and totally changed my life. The afternoon was getting late and we needed to reach Phoenix by evening. However, the ever so kind and patient Marguerite indulged me a quick side trip to Bryce Canyon National Park. We only had time for a quick glance at the beautiful Park and upon exiting the Park entrance station, who should be on duty but my old friend Park ranger J.L. Crawford. Visitors don't stop upon exiting a Park and would never see the ranger, but it just happened that J.L was outside the little entrance station building, for just a moment and that happened to be the moment we passed by. I jumped out of the car, ran over and greeted J.L. as the long lost friend that he was. In a very brief conversation I asked him for advice and suggestions on what I could do to obtain a position in the Park Service. He said that jobs were scarce, maybe two or three job hires a year and very little activity in the movement and promotion of personnel. However, there might be a chance through the "back door" at Carlsbad Caverns National Park. A few rangers had been selected from the ranks of cave guides who were classified as technicians. Also, J.L. had a friend, Jim Eden, who was the Chief Ranger at Carlsbad Caverns National Park. J.L. told me how to apply for a job and said he would provide me with a good recommendation.

Upon returning home from Phoenix, I went to work writing letters to Jim Eden at Carlsbad Caverns. I also applied for any service wide positions in the Park Service but the job picture was extremely bleak. August 25, 1953 I received a letter from Acting Assistant Regional Director Stanley C. Joseph enclosing a Park ranger examination announcement. However, his letter stated, "This examination was held last spring. Since an adequate register (roster of applicants passing the test) has been established for Park rangers it is not expected that this examination will again be announced for some time." There were literally a couple of hundred names on the application register and only five or six people were selected each year. To make the odds even worse, I was eligible for veterans hiring preference, but disabled veterans had the highest employment priority. Where did I muster the perseverance to continue my obsession?

The first ray of hope came in a letter of September 28, 1953 from Assistant Superintendent Thomas E. Whitcraft of Carlsbad Caverns. This letter enclosed a Standard Form 57 (U.S. Government Job Application form) with instruction to complete the form and return it to the Park. He stated, "We have two vacant positions at present, but due to reduced appropriation it is doubtful they can be filled before next spring. I hope that we will be able to help you in a Park Service career and will advise you further after receipt of your form 57."

I can still remember the overwhelming excitement of that day. No job offer and slim hopes of one in the near future, but at least a tiny, tiny bit of hope. I could have screamed with joy, but had no one to share the excitement with. Patricia was an only child and our young son Paul was very attached to his grandmother, so there would be little enthusiasm over us moving away from McNabb, Illinois.

On October 26, 1953 Thomas Whitcraft acknowledged receipt of my completed Form 57 and stated that I was qualified for a tour leader position, but the job picture was unchanged. Tom also suggested that I write to the U.S. Civil Service Commission, Tenth Region, (actually Thirteenth Region) in Denver, Colorado and apply for the next tour leader examination. I followed up on his suggestion and received a form letter from the Civil Service Commission stating that, "There is a possibility the announcement for tour leader will be made early in 1954." and to check back with them.

In the meantime, I maintained a steady stream of correspondence with Carlsbad Caverns and marvel now at the patience, kindness and encouragement received from Assistant Superintendent Tom Whitcraft. For example, in a letter of February 5, 1954 Tom brought me up to date on the employment picture and advised he had information that a tour leader examination would be announced early this year. The examination was announced and on short notice I traveled to Denver, Colorado to take the examination April 30, 1954 and received a perfect score of 100. It really was a very simple test.

Correspondence continued with Carlsbad Caverns and the regional office in Santa Fe, New Mexico. Some of the news was slightly encouraging, but most of it was not. In one letter from Chief Ranger Jim Eden he stated, "Both Bob Barrel and Grant Clark (former seasonal employees with me at Zion National Park) speak very highly of you and I sincerely hope you will be successful in joining our staff." It was an extremely emotional roller coaster for the next several weeks.

CHAPTER III
CARLSBAD CAVERNS NATIONAL PARK
May 1954 - February 1956

On May 3, 1954 the patience and perseverance paid off. A letter from Superintendent R. Taylor Hoskins arrived and the first sentence stated, "We are extremely pleased to have your telegram of May 1 and learn that you will accept the Seasonal Tour Leader position from May 23 to September 1, 1954. The salary was $3,175.00 per annum. Note, this was only a seasonal position but we were willing to take a chance that prior to September 1st a permanent position would become available. Here, once again despite ridiculous odds, my guardian angel was looking after me because ON SEPTEMBER 1ST, THAT LAST DAY OF MY SEASONAL CONTRACT, A PERMANENT JOB DID OPEN AND IT WAS OFFERED TO ME. A tour guide, Wayne Cone, received a promotion and transfer to Yosemite National Park and I was offered his vacated position. In retrospect, all of these unusual and fortunate events were nothing less that a miracle.

Carlsbad Carverns National Park, New Mexico

The work at Carlsbad Caverns was never dull. The several miles of trails in the cave were rather narrow and visitors moved through in a single file position. Every visitors group was escorted through the caverns by three to five Cave Guides, depending upon size of the party. One senior guide was in the lead of each party, one at the rear and other guides moved back and forth through the line visiting with people and answering their questions. Other National Park areas that are also caves, such as Mammoth Cave or Wind Cave may use this same procedure but otherwise this is the only National Park area I'm aware of where each and every visitor is met, in a personal one-to-one with a Park employee. With that close association we were fully aware of the visitors' reaction to the caverns and during the time I worked at Carlsbad I never heard a single word of disappointment or dissatisfaction about their experience in the cave.

Of course the caverns were illuminated by artificial light and it was the job of the lead guide, as we progressed from one point to another on the tour, to turn on the concealed light switch and the rear guide to turn them off. The parties also stopped at several designated locations where guides would take turns talking to the group and explaining features of the cave. We were not permitted to use notes while giving our talks and we did develop very good public speaking skills. The first stop on each tour was just inside the very large entrance of the cave to bring attention to a side cave, which was the resting place for four or five hundred thousand Mexican free-tailed bats. In years past, prior to insecticides, this bat colony numbered in the millions. The bats fly out of the cave each evening to feed on insects and drink water from nearby streams and ponds. In the early morning hours they return to the cave, attach to the cave ceiling and hang upside down to sleep during the daylight hours. This stop at the cave entrance was also a test for some visitors who felt pangs of claustrophobia to determine if they could handle the cave trip.

Another interesting stop was on a fairly steep descent, about mid-point on the tour. Here visitors were invited to sit on the stone wall along each side of the trail while the speaker provided more information about the cave. All of the cave lights were turned out so visitors could experience total, complete darkness. This is why everyone was sitting down, so they wouldn't lose their balance in the dark and fall.

Box lunches were available from the Park Concessionaire at the lunchroom over seven hundred feet below ground. Employees also had their own private lunchroom. I remember one of my favorite bosses, Claude Fernandez, always brought a jalapeno pepper in his lunch and would eat it, seeds and all, just like an apple. Modern, high-speed elevators were also located here to return visitors to the surface several hundred feet above, or bring other visitors down for a tour of the Big Room.

It was a rare visitor indeed who was not awestruck by the size and beauty of the Big Room at the lower level of the cave. The Big Room was almost six hundred feet high and could contain the nation's Capitol Building. The room was so large that visitors seldom experienced feelings of claustrophobia. The trail around the room was a little over a mile in length and filled with a profuse array of cave formations of all size and shape, stalagmites, stalactites, columns, totem poles, flowstone and formations resembling objects. At one point along the trail there was an opening to another lower cave, called the abyss.

Working as a Tour Leader at Carlsbad Caverns National Park was excellent training in public speaking, I think more effective than Toastmasters Club or any public speaking training that I am aware of. We were instructed and did our own individual research on cave information or history, then prepared a narrative, which gave the talk a good, natural flow. We were not permitted to use notes while giving a cave talk and the Chief or Assistant Chief Naturalist frequently monitored the talks to maintain accuracy and quality of information. The Tour Leader, our direct supervisor on each group tour, assigned the several talks to various guides on the tour and we never knew in advance who would give which talk. This procedure insured an impromptu and unstructured quality to the talks and we all became good at our task.

The Park did not have enough housing to accommodate part time employees so for the first several months of my employment we rented an apartment in the city of Carlsbad, about fifteen or twenty miles north of the Park. When I received a permanent position we moved into Park housing. I often volunteered without pay, to assist the Park naturalists by giving the evening "Bat Flight Talk". Thousands, sometimes hundreds of thousands of Mexican Free-tailed bats inhabited a room near the walk-in entrance to the cave. The bats spent daylight hours in the cave sleeping upside down, suspended from the ceiling. In the evening, usually near the time of sunset but on an unpredictable schedule, the bats departed from the cave in search of food and water. They emerged from the cave in an organized, spiral pattern, resembling a dust devil whirlwind, until they reached a certain elevation and peeled off in a horizontal flight.

Carlsbad Carverns National Park, New Mexico

Many visitors came to the Park in the evenings to watch the spectacle of the bat flight. They would sit on the rock wall along the trail entrance, just outside the cave. We entertained these visitors with information about the bats and answered questions until the bats emerged. On occasion, for no obvious reason the bats would show up earlier or later than normal and we had to adjust the length of the talk to fill the void of inactivity or abruptly cut the talk short if the bats flew early.

As mentioned, our annual salary was $3,175.00 and despite the most frugal lifestyle this was insufficient to provide for our needs. Like many other employees I had a second and third part time job. One job was part time driver of the government bus used to haul employees between the city of Carlsbad to and from the Park. Another part time job was giving an evening program about Carlsbad Caverns for the city Chamber of Commerce. A third job was working as a night clerk for the LaCaverna Hotel, a very good, upscale hotel of Spanish architecture and distinguished clients. One of the clients who maintained a suite of rooms for his frequent visits was Horace Albright, first Assistant Director of the newly established National Park Service agency and first Superintendent of Yellowstone, the world's first National Park. After Mr. Albright retired from the National Park Service he was a major stockholder and director of a group of potash mines near Carlsbad. It was a thrill and rare privilege to meet this historic figure and spend evenings or morning breakfast visiting with him.

The area around the Park housing and visitor center area was covered with volcanic rock and desert vegetation. Rocky areas are good habitat for rattlesnakes and we learned to live with them. We never ventured out of the house at night without a flashlight because the snakes liked to sleep on the warm asphalt walkways. We also had scorpions, millipedes, centipedes and various other biting and stinging critters but we also learned to live with them. The way we kept scorpions and centipedes our of our beds was to place each leg of the bed in an empty tin can and make certain the bedding didn't reach the floor.

Park houses were built by the CCC boys during the Great Depression of the 1930s. They were constructed by erecting four wooden walls and then piling stones and mortar against this framework. Once the rock walls reached ceiling height the wooden framework was removed to make another room. Vigas (log rafters) were placed two or three feet apart, spanning the room and then the roof was constructed. The walls of our rock houses were two or three feet thick at the base and tapered off to about a foot thick at the roof level. This resulted in wide windowsills and at night raccoons would sit on the window sills to pick moths and other flying insects off the window screen. It could be quite a shock to walk into a dark room, turn on a light and see this masked face looking in the window.

Close and long-lasting friendships developed with many of our fellow employees and we met some interesting characters. Superintendent R. Taylor Hoskins was a native of Virginia or thereabouts, and one of the first employees of the newly established Shenandoah National Park. His primary activity in this new Park was breaking up the many moonshine operations that existed. Tom Whitcraft, the Assistant Superintendent, was a tall, muscular man who had worked in the newly established Grand Teton National Park. The land for Grand Teton had been purchased secretly and quietly by the John D. Rockefeller family and then given to the U.S. Government for a National Park. Most ranchers and residents of the area deeply resented this land being taken out of private ownership and took their resentment out on the Park employees. Rumor was that Tom Whitcraft had been in a nearby bar in Jackson Hole one evening when some cowboys taunted him about being a government employee. This discussion finally erupted into a brawl and Tom cleaned house on several of the cowboys. However, because of this incident the National Park Service transferred Tom to Carlsbad Caverns.

CHAPTER IV
GRAND CANYON NATIONAL PARK
February 1956 - March 1959

I received a job offer from Chief Ranger Lynn Coffin at Grand Canyon for a promotion to GS-5 at an annual salary of $3,805. We were assigned to quarters #161, a tiny one-bedroom cabin which rented for $8.00 every two weeks. At this time the Federal Government operated on a two-week cycle for paying our wages and collecting miscellaneous fees, which were deducted from our pay.

Grand Canyon had a limited supply of water, which was pumped from a place called Indian Gardens on the Tonto Plateau, along the Bright Angel Trail about 3,000 feet below the canyon rim. Water pressure builds at about one pound of pressure for each two feet of elevation, so pumping water up 3,000 feet required about 1,500 psi (pounds of pressure per square inch) at the Indian Garden pumps. The water was pumped into large storage tanks on the rim.

To make maximum use of the water, the wastewater was reclaimed from the sewage and used to flush toilets and other non-potable uses. As the newest ranger on the staff part of my duties were to fill in for Paul Smith, the night patrol technician, on his days off. Every two hours during the night I had a prescribed route of inspection, plus other areas I felt warranted checking, much of the patrol on foot. There were time clocks that had to be punched at various locations such as the firehouse, jail and sewage treatment plant.

The El Tovar Hotel was also on my route and a highlight of the evening was passing through the kitchen where cooks were preparing the day's meals. Best of all was the heavenly aroma of fresh baked bread and biscuits coming out of the ovens. The cooks were always good about letting me test the fresh baked biscuits with jam or peanut butter. One must keep in mind that the South Rim of the Grand Canyon is at 7,000 feet elevation and winter weather could be pretty cold. Those fresh baked biscuits were much appreciated on those cold and snowy winter nights.

About fifteen months after transfer to Grand Canyon, someone must have transferred out of the Park, as a new ranger entered on duty and

I moved up a notch on the career ladder. My duties changed slightly with a promotion to GS-6 with an annual salary of $4,080. In June of 1958 I was promoted to Pasture Wash Subdistrict Ranger as a GS-7 with a new salary of $4,980, and we moved into a very livable two bedroom residence, #17 with rent of $10.36 every two weeks.

Pasture Wash Subdistrict was a large tract of vacant land, all of the Park south of the Colorado River and from about Hermits Rest, west to the western boundary of the Park. Our main residence remained in Grand Canyon Village, but there was a rustic ranger station at Pasture Wash only occupied for a day or two at a time during patrols of the area. However, the district bordered the famous Havasupai Indian Reservation, so I had the pleasure of making occasional trips into their area. There were only about two hundred members of the tribe and perhaps less than half of them lived in their canyon home. About a half dozen members of the tribe worked for the Park and there was a separate housing area for them, known as the Indian Village, just west of Grand Canyon Village.

Havasupai Village, Arizona

As an example of how cold it could get in the wintertime, we were having a square dance party at the community building one cold winter evening. The participants brought snack food and if we chose to have an alcoholic drink, the bottle was stashed in a snow bank outside the building. On this occasion it was a beautiful winter evening, but very cold. In contrast, it was warm in the building and we could work up a sweat square dancing, so it was refreshing to go outside once in awhile and have a drink from the bottle. The temperature this night must have been below zero and some of the alcoholic beverages didn't actually freeze but the liquid did become super cold, below freezing. A few of the people actually suffered from frostbite of their mouth and throat from drinking the super-cooled beverage.

Grand Canyon N. P.

Suzie Ayres, Superintendent John McLaughlin's secretary, hiked a lot through the forest surrounding the village area on her days off. We had only worked at Grand Canyon a short time when she discovered a body hanging in a tree a couple miles west of the village. Rangers later found from notes in his suitcase that the poor man, from Chicago, apparently came to the Canyon with the intent of committing suicide by jumping from the canyon rim. Apparently he must have looked over the rim and changed his mind, so he hanged himself in a tree. Suzie Ayres was a widow lady with a strange sense of humor, because she said the man was a lost and found item and if not claimed by an owner within sixty days, he's mine.

Before the body could be removed from the tree or touched in any way, the Coconino County Coroner had to be summoned from Flagstaff ninety miles away.   In the meantime I was assigned to guard the body, which might not have been discovered for years except that it happened to be about fifty feet off an unimproved hiking trail used by employees of the Grand Canyon Inn to hike into the village.   It was a balmy early summer day, so I took up a post within sight but some distance from the body, because it was a gruesome sight and didn't smell good either. I was sitting on the ground leaning against a pinion tree and basking in the sun when I observed a man on the trail, coming toward me through the trees, carrying a package that appeared to be laundry he had picked up in the village.

Judging from his staggering walk it was obvious that the man was very much intoxicated. He passed within ten feet of me and I was about to say hello, but didn't because he had not noticed me and I didn't want to startle him. He then stepped off the path a few paces to place his package on a tree stump, removed a half pint whisky bottle from his back pocket, unscrewed the lid and took a healthy drink. Next he unzipped his trousers and relieved himself. After this moment of refreshment he began talking out loud, waving his arms and looking about as if speaking to an audience. He still didn't know that he actually did have an audience of myself and the guy hanging in the tree. He took another swig from the whisky bottle and continued waving, talking, looking about and I was waiting with much anticipation for his reaction when he would cast his eyes on the body hanging in the tree. I wondered how I should respond when this happened, because making my presence known would probably cause him to panic even more and he might have a heart attack.

Despite the hiker remaining in the area for ten or fifteen minutes, he never did see the suicide victim in the tree or myself. Eventually he picked up his bundle from the tree stump and continued his walk in the direction of the old Grand Canyon Inn, which has now been totally removed and no evidence of its existence remains. The site of the Grand Canyon Inn was originally a copper mine and the mining claim was given by President Theodore Roosevelt to one of his Rough Riders from the Spanish American War.

Havasu Falls, Arizona

One of the more interesting characters living at Grand Canyon was Emery Kolb. Emery and his brother Ellsworth Kolb built a home at the head of the Bright Angel trail in 1904 and photographed visitors on mules as they began their trip into the canyon. This was a time of glass plate photography. While the visitors were on their mule trip, one of the boys would hike down the Bright Angel trail to a spring at Indian Gardens, a distance of five miles and three thousand feet below the rim. Here they would process the glass plates in the fresh spring water, produce a photographic print, hike back up the trail and have the print ready for sale when the visitors returned from their mule trip.

The Kolb brothers floated down the Colorado River in 1911 and photographed the experience. They build an auditorium in their home where they charged visitors admission to watch film of their river trip.

Emery Kolb owned a large Packard automobile and each evening at 5:00 pm he would drive to the post office for his mail. His travel route went right past the turnoff to the El Tovar Hotel and the main entrance road to Grand Canyon village. At 5:00 pm this road was chaos with busses returning from their sightseeing trips, the busiest time of the day for visitor traffic, so rangers would be posted to direct traffic. When we saw Emery Kolb coming down the road in his big Packard automobile we stopped traffic in all directions to let him pass because he was a terrible driver and never looked in any direction except straight ahead.

These years were very demanding of the rangers. There were only about ten permanent rangers on the south rim, from the Chief Ranger on down, and we were widely scattered. Stuart Udall was Secretary of the Interior and his family originated from the small community of St. John, Arizona, southeast of Holbrook. Mr. Udall insisted that Park concessioners employ more Native Americans to work during the summer months and the concessioners did a good job of fulfilling his request. We had young Indian men from every tribe in Arizona. Unfortunately these young warriors, some fresh out of the Army, partied every night and when intoxicated they wanted to settle old tribal disputes with members from other tribes. Every night the rangers were breaking up fights, cleaning up vehicle accidents and hauling injured to the hospital or jail. Perhaps I should explain to people unfamiliar with National Parks that the rangers are the Police force, Fire Department for both forest fires and building fires, Search and Rescue, medical and ambulance teams. There are no other public service officials.

A ranger's duty was 24/7 and it was just an unwritten rule that during the busy summer months we didn't leave the Park without the approval of our supervisor, which was seldom denied, but the purpose was that in the event of an emergency too many of us were not absent at the same time. There was no overtime or other compensation made for this and we accepted it as a part of our job. Even Superintendent McLaughlin and his division chiefs checked with each other before leaving the Park on their days off, again to make certain that someone of higher rank was always available.

Superintendent McLaughlin and his staff must have had some discussion on this restriction and decided to relax the unwritten rule. The first weekend for the experiment was the last weekend of June 1956. The weather was beautiful and for the first time the Superintendent, Assistant Superintendent, all division chiefs and assistant division chiefs left the Park and I, the newest and lowest ranking employee, was left in charge of the Park. After all, what could go wrong? There was no threat of a forest fire and if some hiker in the canyon got into trouble we were capable of dealing with it.

However, on June 30, 1956, a beautiful Sunday at 2:20 pm I recorded in my pocket notebook a phone call from Captain Laing, Base Operations, Nellis Air Force Base in Las Vegas, NV the following notation. "Two airliners with one hundred twenty-six passengers, three hours overdue – should be traveling over Painted Desert and Grand Canyon. Any information call extension 21-600 at above address." Soon after I also received a phone call from the Associated Press, Apline 8-4205 in Phoenix, Arizona, "This office would also appreciate any information on the above item."

The Park radio and phone communication systems were very primitive but I contacted the Hopi fire tower, the North Rim District Ranger and Desert View District Ranger to inform them of the Nellis alert. The Park had placed a radio at Grand Canyon Airlines, also known as Red Butte Airport, several miles south of the Park and I was also able to transmit the same information to the Hudgin brothers, who operated the airport. This was just a small, grass strip runway, which provided passenger service to visitors wishing to fly over the Grand Canyon. The Park radio was placed there so that the Hudgen Brothers could notify the Park of forest fires.

I was patrolling Grand Canyon Village and stopped by the Ranger Workshop (rangers at this time made all of the informational signs along roadways) and just as I stepped in the door the radio was crackling, but I was able to make out that it was a message from the Hudgen Brothers. Since the radio communication was poor, I dashed to the Park Administration building and made a phone call to the airport. About midday, Henry and Palen Hudgins had taken passengers on a scenic flight over the canyon and noticed a small wisp of smoke near the mouth of the Little Colorado River and thought it was a small fire created by a lightening strike. However, when they received my message about the missing aircraft they decided to fly over the area to investigate, and upon returning to the airport sent me a message stating that while over the area north of Desert View Watchtower, they flew lower and identified the unique tri-stabilizer tail section of the TWA Constellation aircraft along the shoreline of the Colorado River, near its junction with the Little Colorado River. Some of my notes were as follows, "South of Chuar Butte, Temple Butte, TWA west of mouth of Little Colorado River, NE1/4, Sec 11, T32N, R5E. Crashed 1000 feet above river (this was referring to the United Airlines flight, which had crashed into the side of Chuar Butte and scattered wreckage down the side of the cliff). There were two small fires burning, no survivors, TWA Constellation."

Site of Airliner Crash, Grand Canyon N. P.

I returned a phone call to Nellis Air Force Base to pass along the information and also returned a call to the Associated Press. Then all hell broke loose. Every phone in the Administration Building was ringing off the hook and I was the only person in the building. As soon as possible I phoned Chief Ranger Coffin's residence and fortunately he had just returned to the Park. We rounded up some help to answer the phones and also notified Superintendent John McLaughlin, who also had just returned to the Park.

At this time, this was the largest loss of life in an aircraft accident. What are the odds that two large passenger aircraft would happen to be in exactly the same location, at the exact same elevation, at the exact same time in the wide open, remote airspace of Northern Arizona. As I recall, both aircraft were traveling in the same direction with the TWA Constellation flying just above the United Airlines aircraft. For some reason or other, the pilot of the United Aircraft had radioed and received permission to fly at a higher elevation. Because of the cockpit design, visibility above the United Airliner was very limited and the pilot was totally unaware that a TWA aircraft was only a few feet above. When the United Airliner changed elevation the propellers cut off the tail section of the TWA aircraft, which gyrated to a pancake landing on the beach of the Colorado River. Meanwhile the United Aircraft, now out of control crashed directly into the side of Chaur Butte scattering the wreckage all along the base of the cliff.

CHAPTER V
C & O CANAL NATIONAL HISTORICAL PARK
February 8, 1959 – July 23, 1960

The Chesapeake and Ohio Canal National Historical Park is a big bundle of superb scenery, an area saturated with history, and construction of the canal was an engineering marvel. Many of the original 74 locks, lock houses, aqueducts and dams on the Potomac River still exist, and in fact one of the old lock houses is located on Constitution Avenue, in Washington DC. The canal is 184.5 miles in length, about 60 feet wide at water level and six feet deep, lined with clay to hold water. There were 74 locks, one hundred feet long, I think 16 feet wide, to lift canal boats from an elevation near sea level to 605 feet at Cumberland, MD. There were seven dams built on the Potomac River to divert water into the canal, with twelve feeder locks that regulated the flow of water into the canal, and in a couple locations the canal boats actually shifted to navigate in the river for short distances. The canal passes through a mountain at a place called Paw Paw Tunnel 3,118 feet in length, and eleven beautiful aqueducts were constructed to carry the canal over tributary rivers and streams too large for culverts.

The canal boats were ninety to ninety-five feet long, fourteen and one-half feet wide, drawing about four and one-half feet of water when loaded, the size being limited by the size of the locks. The boats were pulled by mules so a tow path existed parallel to the canal, including over the aqueducts and through the Paw Paw Tunnel. Mules worked six hours a day and a relief set of mules rode in the forward section of the canal boat. The boat captain and family lived in a rear cabin. Incidentally, little children wore a harness attached to a rope or line to keep them from falling overboard and into the canal.

The mules pulled the canal boat at a speed of two miles per hour. Moving a half ton of cargo by horse and wagon was slow and expensive, traveling about twelve to fifteen miles per day. The canal boats could move one hundred tons of cargo about twenty-four miles per day in much greater comfort. It required about four days for a canal boat to travel the full length of the canal, but at this time in history that must have been equal to jet air travel of today. Food for the boat crew was often purchased from the lock tenders who kept chickens, pigs, milk cows and a large garden.

Paw Paw Tunnel, C&O Canal

The most beautiful structure on the C and O Canal is the Monocacy River Aqueduct, built of white granite with the stones fitted together in masterful craftsmanship. This structure is 560 feet in length with seven fifty-four foot arches.

Momocacy Aqueduct, C&O Canal National Historical Park

It boggles my mind to think of accomplishing this highly labor-intensive project, through a wilderness area, with virtually no populated areas from which to recruit labor, horses, equipment and material. At times there were more than six thousand laborers, several hundred horses, mules and oxen working on construction of the canal. Emigrants were hired and each camp tended to be of the same ethnic origin such as Irish, Italian or German. Sometimes there was warfare between camps and camps were also plagued with deadly disease such as cholera.

As the name implies, Chesapeake and Ohio Canal was a concept of building a canal along the Maryland shore of the Potomac River, from the eastern seaboard to Ohio territory. Former President George Washington was a promoter of the canal idea and first president of the Potowmack Company in the late 1700s. The plan was to make the Potomac navigable by building sections of canals along the river at the locations of obstacles such as rapids and waterfalls, Great Falls being one example. However, after a short length of construction the project was dormant until July 4, 1828 when President John Quincy Adams turned the first shovel of dirt to commemorate a new beginning of canal construction. It required twenty-two years (1850) to complete the project at Cumberland, Maryland.

The demise of the canal was caused by a new invention, the "iron horse." The B & O Railroad, Baltimore and Ohio, actually completed track to Cumberland, MD several years before completion of the canal and eventually forced the canal company out of business. Perhaps the railroads could haul goods at less cost, and of course they didn't shut down in the winter months when the canal would freeze over. The final blow was the devastating flood of 1889 (part of the famous Georgetown flood) that caused extensive damage to the canal. Control of the canal company passed to the principal bondholder, the competing B & O Railroad. The United States government eventually acquired the canal property, I think partly due to delinquent taxes owed by the B & O Railroad. I do not know what department of the United States government managed the property at this time, but the Washington Post had editorialized in favor of turning the canal, then thirty years past the end of its commercial life, into a parkway or scenic freeway.

Fortunately, U.S. Supreme Court Justice William O. Douglas had been using the old canal property as a good place for hiking and he had better ideas for use of this historic land. On March 20, 1954 Mr. Douglas began a campaign to save the canal by leading a hike of the full 184 miles from Cumberland, MD to Washington, DC. He challenged the newspaper reporters to accompany him on the hike and several newsmen took him up on the challenge. A dispatch along the way indicated Justice Douglas had won them over as one comment would indicate, "At this point we are torn between a feeling of appreciation to Justice Douglas for luring us into this venture and irritation over the increasingly pathetic condition of our feet. But blisters heal and memories linger." Justice Douglas really saved the historic C & O Canal from oblivion and he was still making these hikes when I arrived on the scene in 1959. I had the honor of participating in one of his last hikes.

Justice Douglas prevailed and the area was transferred to the National Park Service for preservation as a National Historical Park project and development of the unique recreational potential. This northeast quadrant (area north of the Potomac River and Ohio River and east of the Mississippi River) of the United States contained forty-five percent of the nation's population and open space of public land was very limited. The canal sliced through this populated area and one could hike or bike this historic and scenic trail for 184 miles without an obstruction, stop light, crossroad or fence.

Supreme Court Justice William O. Douglas, C&O Canal

The original staffing of the new Park had just begun before my arrival on March 8, 1959 and I was the fourth member of the original staff. We were Superintendent Edwin M. Dale, Secretary Martha Cosgrove, Chief of Maintenance and myself, the Lone Ranger. Superintendent Dale had just been transferred from the then undeveloped ghost and slum town of Harpers Ferry. His career prior to that was Chief Ranger of the Blue Ridge Parkway. Sam Weems, an iconic figure in the eastern National Parks, had been Superintendent of the Blue Ridge all of his career. Most of the employees were born and raised Southern Gentlemen, almost a cult group.

Superintendent Mack Dale was a good guy but we came from entirely different backgrounds and I thought he was kind of stuffy, a little overbearing and posturing the role of a southern gentleman. I thought of him as a Professional Confederate. One morning, during deer hunting season in Virginia, the newspaper reported that a couple of hunters had been accidentally shot and injured by other hunters mistaking them for deer. I used this opportunity to give Mack a fun poke and said, "If those damn rebels could shoot straight they would be killing rather than wounding each other." Boy, this really set him off and I had to endure a half hour lecture on the marksmanship of the Confederate Army.

On another occasion my wife Patricia was riding with Mrs. Eloise Dale and her mother TT to a coffee at Harpers Ferry. Along the way they passed one of the countless Civil War battlefields in the area and Eloise said, "This is where they buried the Yankees and just plowed the rebels under." Patricia thought she was joking and laughed, but it was no joke with these southerners. This was a battlefield north of the Mason-Dixon Line and the implication, and maybe fact, was that the southern dead were not treated with the same respect as Yankee burials. We were having observances of the Civil War Centennial at this time but it was obvious that many of the battles were still being refought over and over in the minds of these residents.

Prior to my arrival as the first National Park Service ranger assigned to the canal, Sargent Fallon from the National Capitol Park Police, a branch of the National Park Service, occasionally patrolled the canal on his motorcycle. There were no boundary markers to define the Park and in fact no one really knew where the boundaries were. The only thing we had were copies of old, original plat maps created by the Chesapeake and Ohio Canal Company almost one hundred and fifty years ago, with survey notes and boundaries defined by "Meets and Bounds".

These surveys tied to physical objects like trees, fence posts or rocks. For example, the survey might run from a large oak tree, marked with a blaze, West 50 degrees North, 30 seconds South, for sixteen chains (a chain was sixty-six feet long) to a large boulder, thence West 10 degrees, 45 seconds North, for nine chains, to the corner post of a fence. The problem was that few of these original landmarks still existed. There was a State historical sign at one location where a section of the boundary was described as, "a distance as fur as an arrow can be flung from a bow".

The U.S. government property, once part of the C & O Canal, included a lot of the old lock houses located at each canal lock, where the lock tender and family lived. Some of these houses had been rented to the public for vacation homes or permanent dwellings. Most of these surviving houses were built of stone or brick, they were small but quite picturesque and often located in very scenic locations along the Potomac River. I discovered that most of these renters were paying a trivial rental fee, some had not paid rent for years and I even found a couple of houses that the government didn't know existed. One of my jobs was to define the land area to be included with each rental house, establish the terms of occupancy and establish a reasonable rental rate.

In the western, more remote sections of the canal, there were a couple of active moonshine stills operating. I knew who these people were and they knew me but we didn't bother each other. I maintained a friendly relationship with these people because they helped me protect the property from squatters and vandalism. I had my hands full patrolling 184 miles of real estate by myself.

I had my first experiences with racial discrimination while living in Maryland. On one occasion I had been sent to a meeting of Park rangers at Everglades National Park in Florida. On my return trip home I rode a bus from Homestead, Florida to the airport in Jacksonville, Florida. At a bus stop some black people boarded the bus and I had been paying little attention to activities, but we traveled only a short distance when the bus driver slammed on the brakes, stood up, turned and just screamed at the new passengers. I was jolted out of my stupor by his behavior and didn't know what was going on. It turned out that some of the black passengers who had just boarded the bus had taken seats only part of the way toward the rear of the bus and they were supposed to sit in the vary last seats. This was my first encounter with racial discrimination and the episode was embarrassing to me.

This was a time prior to the great Civil Rights movement, Martin Luther King, Governor Maddox of Georgia and freedom marches. Hagerstown, Maryland was situated just north of the Mason-Dixon line and there was a lot of racial discrimination in town. However, it was a quiet thing. Black people were not rebelling and so it just went on without notice. We had joined a large Lutheran church in Hagerstown and were warmly received, but I was curious why there were no black people in the congregation. We were told that this was a white people's church and blacks were not welcome - another cultural shock and embarrassment for us. How could Christian people, in church of all places, practice racial discrimination?

Maryland is a place of exquisite beauty, reeking with history and at that time I was a student of civil War history. Hagerstown was a beautiful and very livable city. Even then, prior to interstate highways, Washington, DC was only an hour or two away in driving time. Countless historic sites, including Harpers Ferry, Gettysburg and Antietam Battlefields surrounded us, and historic Philadelphia, the location of our regional office, was about one hundred and seventy-five miles away. The Dutch food in little towns surrounding Philadelphia left lifetime memories. We also visited Baltimore, Fort McHenry, the U.S. Naval Academy at Annapolis, Shenandoah and Great Smoky Mountains National Parks. The rolling hills of western Maryland with apple orchards and wooded hillsides covered with hardwood trees, magnolia, dogwood and boxwood were a picture right out of Currier and Ives.

So why was I so unhappy? I have never been so homesick in my life and in retrospect I feel so bad about the negative attitude I had – not making the most of this unusual experience and instead making misery of this special opportunity. As one of my favorite expression goes, pain is inevitable but misery is optional. At least I learned a valuable lesson, which is to have a positive attitude about one's situation in life, take advantage of opportunity and make the most of life.

The problem of living in Maryland was the big contrast to living in the western states. The lack of public land to roam, the crowds of people everywhere we went and always standing in long lines. The closer you were to Washington, DC, the greater the number of people who worked for the government, and they were very class conscious, concerned with what your grade level was, who you worked for and how influential you were. It seemed that everyone I met in the National Park Service had a goal of transfer to a big western Park and I had given all that up to move east. The sickening thought for me, was that I had made a big mistake moving east. Now, will I ever have another chance to live and work in the west again? The odds didn't look good. I was behaving like a spoiled brat and now when visiting the east I appreciate the beauty and charming living conditions.

Harpers Ferry was another newly created National Park area and located at the confluence of the Shenandoah and Potomac Rivers, across the Potomac from the C & O Canal. I frequently stopped to visit a ranger friend at Harpers Ferry and have lunch together when I was on patrol in the area. The very picturesque town was perched on a steep hillside but was pretty much a ghost town at the time, and many of the old historic stone homes and business buildings were vacant ruins and in disrepair.

Harpers Ferry National Historical Park

At this time at Harpers Ferry, a crew of archeologists was excavating the site of the old government armory that had been raided by John Brown just prior to the Civil War. In the raid by John Brown the armory building, where firearms were manufactured, had been burned to the ground. The archeological exploration was accomplished by digging trenches in a grid like pattern to locate the exact imprint of the building foundation. Some of the trenches were a solid mass of rusty, bent and twisted firearms, entangled and molded together by heat from the fire. The last time these weapons had been seen was the night John Brown was here and it was thrilling and fascinating to see history unfold.

At other times I would schedule my patrol trips to have lunch with the employees at Antietam Battlefield, also located adjacent to the C & O Canal. The elderly superintendent had once worked at Glacier National Park in Montana, with an old friend of ours from Carlsbad Caverns National Park, Tom Whitcraft. The Park historian, Bob Lagerman was an interesting fellow and good historian, but really out of his element in dealing with the public because he was a very private, introverted person and I think he suffered some psychological damage during service in WWII. Bob was a husky fellow, somewhat of a loner, and a quiet, reclusive person, but still friendly if you were patient and earned his confidence. I gradually earned his friendship by asking questions about the battle of Antietam and he taught me a lot about the history of the battle.

While working in Maryland, one of the most exciting events I participated in was the National Governors Conference at Glacier National Park in 1960, hosted by Montana Governor Hugo Aarnson, known as the galloping Swede. How could I have ever dreamed that some day I would return to Glacier as the Superintendent. When I did return in 1974, Hugo Aarnson was living in the Columbia Falls Veterans Home.

This conference would be an incomprehensible event today, a National Governors Conference including both political parties, not just Republican or Democratic governors, but all fifty states were included. One Park ranger was selected from each state, if possible, to be an escort and chauffeur for the governor of his State. In June 1960 I was detailed to be an escort for Governor J. Millard Tawes of Maryland, certainly a coveted assignment.

This governors conference was a major news media event, even by today's standards and many famous news people were on hand, including Edward R. Murrow. His most notable claim to fame was standing up to Senator Joe McCarthy of Wisconsin and identifying him as a phony communist fighter. McCarthy had ruined the careers and lives of hundreds of famous people by holding senate hearings and claiming them to be communists. The U.S. Congress, the news media and everyone else were completely intimidated and mute with the fear of attracting McCarthy's attention and bullying. Edward R. Murrow had the courage to take on Senator McCarthy and expose him for the bully he was.

A small, select circle of governors had greater national stature and significance and stood out from the crowd. A prominent list of names were Nelson A. Rockefeller of New York, Mark O. Hatfield of Oregon, Edmund G. "Pat" Brown of California, father of the current Governor Brown, Orval E. Faubus of Arkansas and Abraham A. Ribicoff of Connecticut. The events and speeches were closely watched and recorded because several of these governors were potential candidates for President.

General Motors sent fifty brand new Cadillac cars for each ranger to use in chauffeuring our respective governors to whatever destination he wanted, regardless of the time, night or day. Frank Anderson, Superintendent of Harpers Ferry, West Virginia was also detailed to this event and we traveled together by train from the east coast. The trip required two or three days but it was an exhilarating experience. I especially remember the dome cars of the Great Northern Railway and the luxurious club car at the end of the train. We could sit in living room style furniture, arranged in a home like setting and enjoy a cool drink while viewing the passing scenery.

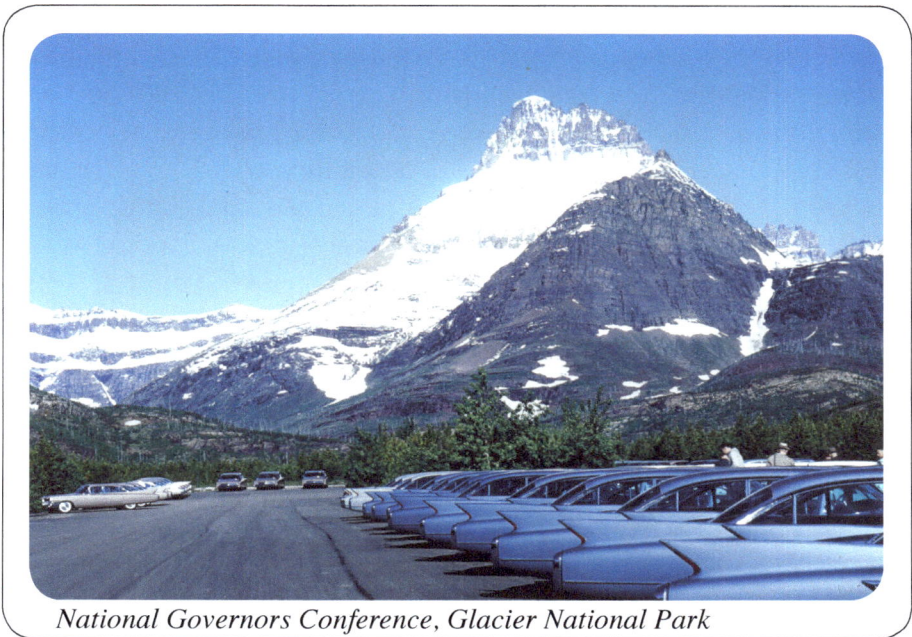

National Governors Conference, Glacier National Park

We disembarked from the train at West Glacier, where we checked in at

Park Headquarters with Chief Ranger Gordon Bender and his assistant Stan Spurgeon. I would eventually work for Stan Spurgeon when he was Chief Ranger at Rocky Mountain National Park. In the future I would also work with Gordon Bender in the Midwest Regional Office in Omaha. Later in the evening most of us assembled at Eddy's Bar and Café in Apgar, at the foot of Lake McDonald and near West Glacier. The big event on television this night was the world heavyweight boxing match between Ingemar Johansson of Sweden and Max Schmelling of Germany. By the way, Eddy's Café is still in business and looks much as it did over fifty years ago, and the owner's son Neil Brewster worked in Glacier when I was Superintendent. Most of the Governors Conference was to take place at Many Glacier Hotel on the east side of the Park but a snow storm had closed Logan Pass and forced us to remain in West Glacier - and this was in the month of June!!!

One afternoon on my day off, I was driving in downtown Hagerstown and as I turned a corner to the right, there was Senator John F. Kennedy standing on the corner talking to a couple of pedestrians. He was just a few feet away from the car so I had a good look at him and thought how I liked the things I had been reading about him.

I had pretty much resigned myself to the fact that it would probably be a long time until I had an opportunity to transfer back to a western National Park. Usually an employee had to be in the present position about three to five years before consideration for a transfer, and we had only been at the C & O Canal for about fifteen months. Another issue at this time was that the receiving Park had to pay the transfer costs for an incoming employee directly from their operating budget, so the practical thing was to recruit employees from nearby Parks and reduce the transfer cost. One more obstacle was that at my grade level, a GS-7, employees were rarely recruited outside the regional boundaries.

Despite all of these obstacles, on July 23, 1960 I received a phone call from Lynn Coffin, Chief Ranger at Grand Canyon National Park, offering me a supervisory ranger position with a sizeable promotion. I would have been thrilled to death to make such a move with a demotion. Once again that guardian angel was looking out for me and anyone not working within the Federal Government at this time could not fully comprehend the odds of making such a transfer.

CHAPTER VI
GRAND CANYON NATIONAL PARK – The 2nd Time
July 23, 1960 – June 3, 1962

Upon our return to Grand Canyon on July 26, 1960 we not only returned home, but with a nice promotion to GS-9, a salary of $6,435.00 came with the transfer. We were assigned to the same house, quarters #17, that we moved from a little over a year earlier. The rental rate was $14.50 bi-weekly, or a little more than $30.00 per month. On February 5, 1961 we had acquired enough points to qualify for one of the new Mission 66, three-bedroom, ranch-style homes. The new house was quarters #377, which rented for $34.18 bi-weekly plus $2.00 bi-weekly for the single car garage.

West Rim Viewpoint, Grand Canyon N. P.

I cannot adequately express the disbelief and happiness of returning to Grand Canyon. It was something of a "born again" experience, because I left Grand Canyon with a "taken for granted" attitude and returned with exuberance, elated and greatly anticipating every day. I was happy in every fiber of my body. I had taken a class in oil painting at Dana College and learned that in a painting the brightest part of a scene would be located next to the darkest of dark. This turned out to also be the experience of my life. How fortunate I was to have this great lesson of value for the remainder of my life.

Prior to "Mission 66", a massive renovation of facilities was taking place in commemoration of the National Parks fiftieth anniversary in the year 1966. Prior to this time Visitors Centers didn't exist. Most Parks had dark, dingy buildings hidden away in some remote corner and referred to as museums, but most of them were not designed for public visitation, really just a place to store stuff like a butterfly collection, rocks, Indian pottery or skeletons. Roads were narrow and in poor condition, originally built for horse-drawn vehicles and Model T cars. Campgrounds were designed for tent camping and now visitors were bringing house trailers. To provide technical support for the overwhelming construction activities, a new branch of the Service was created with offices in Philadelphia and San Francisco, called the Eastern and Western Offices of Design and Construction.

A new Visitor Center (the title Visitor Center was also a new innovation) with a few offices had recently been constructed about a mile east of Grand Canyon Village. Water and sewer lines had been built from the village and even extended a short distance beyond the building so that they could be connected to facilities planned in the future. The ground was almost solid rock, Kaibab Limestone covered with a thin layer of dirt, so digging a trench below frost line required drilling, blasting and jackhammers. On this particular day construction crews were digging utility trenches east of the Visitor Center to connect with a new water tank near Mather Point and work was approaching the point of connecting to the previously installed lines.

On this day I was showing a new ranger, Vince Hefti, around the Park as an orientation and for a brief moment left him at the information desk of the new Visitor Center while I completed some other necessary task. A few minutes later a huge explosion took place and the Visitor Center was bombarded with hundreds of rocks. The side of the building looked like a war zone, most of the windows broken and several big rocks came through the roof. One boulder about the size of a basketball dropped through the roof and landed on the floor in front of the information desk, inches from where Vince had been standing. It was a miracle that no one was injured.

The construction crew had been blasting a trench in the rocky ground, but as the work approached the previously built trench the dynamited rock blew laterally in a line of least resistance and in the direction of the building, rather than upward. One rock about the size of a baseball went screaming past the front of the Visitor Center and struck the side of a car in the parking lot about a hundred feet away. Fortunately no one was injured, but it was quite an exciting introduction to the Park for ranger Vince Hefti.

Today some rangers are highly trained and designated as Law Enforcement Rangers, but at this time we had minimal law enforcement training and it was a policy to keep firearms, if we happened to be carrying one, from public view. We didn't want visitors to feel they were in a threatening environment and wanted the rangers to be friendly and approachable. At Grand Canyon we had a deputy sheriff of Coconino County, Bud Dunnagan, as more of a political compromise giving a higher profile and recognition that the state of Arizona did have some jurisdiction in the Park. Chief Ranger Lynn Coffin didn't like this arrangement one little bit and pretty much avoided contact with our deputy sheriff. However, Bud and I didn't live far apart, I liked him and we worked well together. Because of this relationship Chief Ranger Coffin designated me to handle law enforcement cases on the South Rim.

We had two judges in the community, a Justice of the Peace who handled the county law enforcement cases and a U.S. Magistrate who handled our federal law enforcement cases. Actually, rangers were deputized by the County Sheriff and could take cases to either court. The U.S. Magistrate was very fond of Native Americans and if we brought one to his court the case was usually dismissed or treated with a very light sentence. On the other hand, the Justice of the Peace was also the Fred Harvey Company personnel officer and if we brought a Fred Harvey employee into his court they were also released or given a minimum penalty.

Bud and I soon figured out how to work the system and receive what we thought to be proper treatment in court. If I arrested a Native American I would hand the case over to Bud to be handled in the Justice of the Peace Court. On the other hand, if Bud arrested a Fred Harvey Company employee he would hand the case over to me and I would take the person to U.S. Magistrate Court. This was not really a kosher form of justice but we were just doing the best we could to achieve what we thought was proper treatment in court.

One beautiful summer evening, Joe and Marie Rumburg and their children were visiting our home and I received a phone call from Joe Ernest, manager of the Fred Harvey Hopi House. A cabin maid had cleaned a cabin at Grand Canyon Village Inn (no longer in existence) and when making the bed discovered an overnight bag containing thousands of dollars. The bag was placed in a safe at the Hopi House until reclaimed by the owner. Early in the evening a young couple did return to the Park to claim their bag. However, a problem arose when the couple could not produce any identification. After a couple of hours Mr. Ernest phoned me at home. Joe Rumberg, who was my boss, went with me the El Tovar Hotel to meet Mr. Ernest and resolve the lost luggage issue.

We all assembled in a room behind the check-in counter at the El Tovar Hotel and met the nice looking young couple. They were from Houston, Texas, had just been married and were on their honeymoon. The young man said he had sold his business and this was the reason for the large sum of money in the overnight bag. We asked for their home address which they supplied but here another problem arose – the address given was a vacant lot. The situation was getting a little dicey. The girl said she had left her drivers license in the car so I accompanied her to the car, but after rummaging around she couldn't find the license and we walked back to the hotel. When entering the lobby, I asked her to empty the contents of her purse on a coffee table. There was nothing unusual in the purse so we rejoined the others.

Now the young man wanted to return to their car, parked at quite a long distance from the hotel and the girl joined us. It was getting dark and my nervous system was on high alert as the three of us walked to the car. I was dressed in a T-shirt and Levi pants, and not even carrying a jack knife so I walked closely behind the two watching for any sudden move on their part. When we reached their car they again rummaged around and I kept between them so there could not be any secret communications between them. That may have saved my life as I will later explain.

After a short while I requested that we all go back to the hotel and finish our task. I wanted to keep them focused on the hope of returning their bag and money and not doing anything foolish. As we returned to the room my boss, Joe Rumberg was on the phone with the Houston Police Dept. He had just hung up the phone when the police called back. One of the officers remembered something, checked some records and realized that we had a robber on our hands; this was his third time offense and he would automatically be sentenced to prison for life. Furthermore, the man was known to be armed and dangerous. The Houston Police asked us to arrest the couple, impound their vehicle and they would send a couple of officers as soon as possible to take them back to Texas. None of us had a weapon of any kind on hand, but just at that moment Dan Kusch, the Fred Harvey Company night watchman happened to be walking by in the hallway and I quickly briefed him on the situation. He always carried a gun, so with his assistance the young couple were placed under arrest.

We placed their car in the firehouse for the night and the next day the Houston Police arrived. In searching the vehicle they did find a firearm. Now back to the previous night when I walked the girl to the car. What I think happened was that she realized we might search the car, so when she was rummaging around she hid the gun. Then when I walked both of them to the car the second time, the man was intent on getting the gun but couldn't find it because the girl had moved it. What saved my butt was keeping myself between them so she couldn't reveal to him where she had hidden the gun.

One historic event we witnessed while living at Grand Canyon was the construction of Glen Canyon Dam, upstream on the Colorado River, which must have begun about 1960. The site was very isolated, about twenty miles east of U.S. Highway 89 and access was via terribly dusty, sandy, washboard roads that could rattle your teeth, with no gas stations, stores or restaurants between Grand Canyon and Page except a trading post at Cameron. The town of Page was nothing more than a trailer village. Our friends, Jack and Betty Settles, were transferred from Grand Canyon to Page by the Babbit Company to establish a grocery store, which was located in a couple double-wide house trailers. There was not a bank in Page so when Jack and Betty closed the store at night they had to take the money box home and stash it under the bed. Page was quite a freewheeling town of construction workers, but I don't recall news of serious crimes - probably because if anyone did commit a crime, there was really no escape because it would take a long time to drive those sandy, washboard roads to elude the law.

At this time workers hadn't completed the diversion tunnels for the Colorado River and the only crossing over the river was a footbridge for the workers to cross from one side to the other. Let me tell you about this bridge. Steel cables were threaded through the ends of chain link fence, which was strung a considerable distance across and about fifteen hundred feet above the river. The chain link fence served as the tread and sides of the bridge, so you could look directly down and see giant earth moving equipment, which at that elevation appeared to be tiny toys. The thrill of walking on this bridge was not only the visual impact below, but the bridge would sway and bounce up and down with your footsteps.

The neighboring Hopi and Navajo Indian tribes held several special dances throughout the summer months to commemorate events or solicit a blessing of the spirits for rain, good crops and well-being. We occasionally attended these events and since very few non-native Americans attended, we were welcome. One of the Hopi dances reenacted a raid by Navajo warriors on their village. In this original raid an unmarried Hopi girl had been on the rooftop making her hair into a roll like buns that covered her ears and this hairstyle identified her as a single girl. She had finished one side of her head when she could see the Navajo warriors approaching and cried out an alarm. The dance commemorated this event and when the alarm was sounded we all had to run into the nearest home or face the possibility of being struck by switches carried by a Kachina. We remained in the home, with door shut and window shades pulled until the all clear. In the meantime, owners of the home offered food, usually mutton stew.

Another dance we found fascinating was the Snake Dance. This usually took place in a courtyard with the area almost entirely surrounded by homes. Prior to the dance men would scour the countryside gathering up live snakes, mostly rattlesnakes. These snakes would be released in the center of the courtyard and dancers following a beat of the drums would scoop up a snake and actually place it in his mouth. Meanwhile a Kachina, I think it was the Wolf Kachina, would dance alongside and

54

flick a feather in front of the snake to direct attention away from the dancer. In another part of the dance, the dancers would scoop up the snakes, now scattered about the courtyard and carry as many as eight snakes, one between each pair of fingers. The grip was close behind the snakes head to prevent it from biting the dancer. Part of the excitement for spectators was standing around the courtyard next to the buildings as a hundred snakes are looking for escape, slithering toward you with no place to back away. After the dance the snakes were gathered up by the dancers who departed from the area to all points of the compass and the snakes were released. I think the belief was that scattering the snakes in all directions would bring rain back to the village. I feel fortunate that we were privileged to witness these events before roads were improved and the general public became aware of the dances, which brought more restrictions.

Hopi House, Arizona

In the spring of 1962 a national Superintendents conference was held at Grand Canyon. Incidentally, it was at this conference that Secretary of the Interior Udall fired Conrad Wirth as Director of the National Park Service and appointed George Hartzog in his place. Connie Wirth had convinced the U.S. Congress to fund his Mission 66 program that brought the National Park Service out of the dark ages and he was very popular with the Superintendents, so this was not a happy occasion.

I was delivering a message to someone at the meeting during a break, and ran into old friend Superintendent Fred Fagergren from Petrified Forest National Monument. It was a beautiful sunny day and while we were standing outside in front of the community building, Fred casually mentioned that he had a vacant Chief Ranger position and had requested my name on the register of candidates. I didn't want to show my true feelings and disappoint my friend, but I was not thrilled with the news. I felt an obligation to remain in my present job a bit longer and Petrified Forest was not much of an enticement for creature comforts. On the other hand, the position was designated for an upgrade when the new headquarters at Painted Desert was completed in a couple months.

CHAPTER VII
PETRIFIED FOREST NATIONAL MONUMENT
June 3, 1962 – May 22, 1965

When the formal transfer offer arrived from Superintendent Fagergren I reluctantly accepted the position. This tour of duty at Grand Canyon had been a life-changing experience, we were happy and I was indebted to my boss, so it was hard to leave.

The new Park headquarters at Painted Desert had not been completed so we moved into temporary quarters at Rainbow Forest, at the south end of the Park. We enjoyed living in the old CCC-constructed stone building, quarters #51, as it was cool, comfortable and situated in interesting surroundings. The rental rate was $23.50 bi-weekly. About three months later the new facilities at Painted Desert were completed and we moved into new quarters #202 and the rental rate was $27.00 bi-weekly. It is interesting to note that the quarters rental charge was broken down as follows: net shelter = $18.69, water (flat rate) $1.48, garbage disposal = $0.58, fuel oil (adjustable) = $5.32, carport = $1.00. On July 7, 1963 rent was increased to $30.00 bi-weekly, but then for some unexplained reason on May 10, 1964 rent was reduced to $24.00 plus the same utility rates.

The new development included eighteen single-family homes, a large, two-story administration building with offices on the second floor and Visitor Center on the first floor. A wing of the building also contained several apartments for single employees. There was a large maintenance building and storage area, and a movie theater for visitor interpretive programs, but employees also used it as an entertainment center. There was also a new grade school because the nearest town was twenty-five or thirty miles away. Fred Harvey Company also had a new concession building with gift shop, restaurant and gas station, and a small mobile home park for employees.

When these new facilities opened, the Park staff almost doubled in size and on August 4, 1963 I received the promised salary increase to GS-11 at $8,045.00 per annum. As salary increased so also did deductions, such as retirement contributions, federal and state income tax, and life and health insurance, so sometimes pay increases weren't all that they seemed to be.

Petrified Forest National Monument is located in both Navajo and Apache Counties of Arizona and borders the Navajo Indian reservation on the north. Prior to the construction of Interstate 40, the old U.S. Highway 66 followed close to the rim of the Painted Desert and an old Fred Harvey Comapny hotel, the Painted Desert Inn, was still standing vacant on a high overlook with a beautiful view of the desert. Remnants of the old highway were still evident, just north of the new headquarters development, and I recall a single U.S. Highway 66 sign on a steel post was still standing on the shoulder of the old road.

Petrified Forest National Monument, Arizona

During our tour of duty at Petrified Forest, Stuart Udall was Secretary of the Interior. The Udall family originated from the picturesque little neighboring town of St. John, Arizona, also the county seat for Apache County. Consequently, the Park received a lot of attention from Mr. Udall and we benefited greatly from that association. For one thing, the Park was staffed more heavily than needed. It was closed at the entrance stations each night to protect against the stealing of valuable petrified wood. The old Park headquarters and housing area were located at Rainbow Forest, at the southern end of the Park. When Interstate Hwy. 40 was built, the National Park Service felt that the headquarters should be relocated at the northern end, near the Painted Desert and the new highway. Thanks to Mr. Udall, this new complex was built and all of it was designed by the famous architectural firm of Alexander-Neutra.

Richard Neutra gave this project his personal attention and the housing area was patterned after an Indian Pueblo village, with homes clustered in a rectangular arrangement to form enclosed courtyards as protection from the wind and weather. The design was great but the quality of construction and workmanship was poor. The walls were plain, naked concrete cinder block, unfinished on both sides. Cinder block is porous and when the wind would blow, which was often, it would actually drive fine grains of sand right through the walls. This drafty situation also made it difficult to heat the house during cold weather. To reduce the invasion of wind and sand in the house, I tacked a large sheet of plastic to the inside top of an exterior wall and rolled a 2 x 4 in the bottom of the plastic to anchor it against the wall. However, when the wind was blowing fairly hard the sheet of plastic would billow out like a sail, but at least the sand would collect along the wall, at the bottom.

The climate at Petrified Forest was frequently windy, with little vegetation growing in this high prairie country to impede the force of wind. Huge piles of tumbleweed would accumulate in any walled area, the winters were cold and the summers were hot. Despite inhospitable surroundings and climate, the people were friendly and we had good times together. In addition to the scenic attractions of the petrified wood and the painted desert, the area had many prehistoric and archeological sites with numerous Indian pictographs and petroglyphs. Pictographs are images painted on the rock surface and petroglyphs are images etched into the rock by chipping with another pointed rock. The Park bordered the Navajo Indian reservation with many opportunities to explore the history and culture of the Native American people. Areas like Window Rock, the Navajo Tribal capitol, Canyon de Chelly National Monument, Hubbel Trading Post National Historic Park and Chaco Canyon Cultural National Historic Park were particularly fascinating areas to visit. Phoenix was also only about a three hour drive and a fun place to go during the cold winter months.

During the summer of 1962, Patricia and the boys rode the Santa Fe Railroad to Illinois for a visit with her parents. While they were gone, ranger Joe Kastellic and I took a camping trip in my old pickup truck to Chaco Canyon, north of Gallup, New Mexico. The Superintendent Robert Heyder and his wife Kathy were my friends from when he and I were co-workers at Grand Canyon. We drove backcountry dirt roads all the way across the Navajo reservation and in some places the road was nothing more than a trail, even passing through barbed wire fence gates in some places. We crossed the forested area of the Lukachukai Mountains and a beautiful, picturesque valley on the east side.

The entrance to Chaco Canyon was a dirt road and not a good place to be in wet weather, but we made the trip without incident and had a great trip. Chaco Canyon is the most interesting archeological site I have ever visited. The architecture and construction of the buildings is very sophisticated. In the building walls, stones were selected and placed in the wall to achieve a color pattern or a size pattern. The large building known as Pueblo Bonito, built in the late 1400s to early 1500s, was the largest apartment building in the world for over two hundred years. In recent years, archeologists have learned a great deal more about the culture of Chaco Canyon and now believe that Pueblo Bonito was more of a religious site associated with astronomy, movement of the sun, moon and stars. The building and the alignment of the several villages are perfectly north - south, east - west.

Chaco Canyon, Pueblo Bonito, Arizona

A large section of a cliff adjacent to Pueblo Bonito broke away and fell onto the village, destroying part of it. I think this happened around 1950. The interesting thing is that the pueblo Indians, at the time they lived here, had identified the problem and built rock walls around the base of this threatening rock to stabilize it and it worked for about five hundred years.

A big problem in the protection of Petrified Forest was the pilfering of petrified wood by Park visitors as a small souvenir, but with thousands of visitors the loss becomes substantial. Hundreds of pounds of petrified wood were leaving the Park each month. Visitors were quite creative in how they would hide these chunks of rock - in the spare tire, the dog food, one rock was even found in a pot of baked beans and the rangers became very skillful in finding the contraband.

The roads through Petrified Forest, except Interstate 40 and Arizona Highway 180, were closed each night at sundown and blocked by gates to protect against the stealing of valuable petrified wood. However, at least one commercial thief of the valuable petrified wood found a way around this protection. Ranger Joe Kastellic had noticed that on nights of full moon, a pickup truck was often parked near a bridge over a dry streambed on Arizona Highway 180, which bisected the southern corner of the Park. We eventually recorded a description of the pickup truck and license plate. On a day after one of these full moons, Joe and I investigated the area and found footprints and the track of a two-wheeled cart in sand of the dry streambed. We noticed the left footprint had a twisted imprint and concluded the intruder had a leg impairment. There were also imprints of a walking stick to further support our conclusion. We made a couple of plaster casts of the footprints. We also measured the cart tracks and were even able to determine the wheel diameter because where the cart straddled little mounds of sand, the axle would level the top of some mounds higher than the axle. At the end of the trail we found a rock hammer, rock chisel and a pair of leather gloves. Apparently our rock thief entered the Park as a visitor, found this remote place where he could select choice, jewelry quality petrified wood, stockpile it and then return on moonlit nights to retrieve the collection. Even back in the 1960s, certain types of petrified wood known as picture wood were sold for $9.00 per pound.

We contacted F.B.I. agent E.L. Boyle from Phoenix, gave him the evidence we had collected and he arrested a prominent rock dealer in Phoenix. The cart that we had identified was even parked in front of his rock shop loaded with petrified wood. Unfortunately, the United States Attorney was overloaded with cases and didn't want to prosecute our case, so the culprit was given a warning, a real scare and the theft of petrified wood came to an end, so mission accomplished.

The most interesting person I met while working at Petrified Forest was Nellie Nampeyo, a famous potter and daughter of another famous potter from First Mesa of the Hopi reservation. We visited Nellie at her home on the reservation one time and memory is fading, but I believe it was in or near the village of Polacca. The prestigious Heard Museum in Phoenix even has a room dedicated to the Nampeyo family. In the late 1800s, Nellie's mother asked her husband to collect pottery shards lying about the ancient ruins and she then copied the designs to her creations. This was known as Sityatki Polychrome.

Nellie's daughter and her husband, as I remember their name was Lucas, worked for the Park concessioner's gift shop at Rainbow Forest, at the southern entrance of the Park. Nellie, now a great-grandmother without a grey hair on her head, came to live with her daughter during the summer months and to make and sell pottery on the front patio of the concession gift shop. Living as a neighbor provided the good fortune of meeting Nellie and she permitted me to make 8mm movie film of the entire process of making pottery. I also made tape recordings of an interview with her, which was a fascinating history of early life on the reservation. I gave both the 8mm film and tape recordings to Petrified Forest as historical documents. After filming the pottery-making process, I also purchased a couple of the pots which Nellie autographed.

Every ingredient of Nellie's pottery, including the decoration, was made from natural elements, including the dried sheep manure used in the baking process. The clay was gathered near her home at First Mesa, she said at the base of the cliff where she lived. The black paint, applied by a brush made from the tip of a yucca leaf, was made from wild bean plants. Leaves of the bean plant were boiled in water over a bonfire for a long time until the residue was thick. The yellow paint color was made by grinding a certain rock into a fine powder and dissolving it in water.

Chaco Canyon Pueblo Ruins, Arizona

Nellie began making the pot by rolling clay between her hands to form a thin rope which she then formed into a coil, making the shape of the pot. Occasionally she took an old pot shard and using the convex side, she smoothed the clay coil, inside and out, to form a smooth surface.

These newly formed pots were then allowed to dry for a few days, then a thin coat of clay was washed over the entire pot and I believe this was called the "slip" coat. When the pot was again dry she painted a design from memory, free hand, without measuring or laying out a pattern. Her paintbrush was a yucca leaf, which she chewed the tip of to produce fine fibers. The painting process was a most fascinating step because she simply held the pot in her left hand, and turning the pot slowly, she applied the paint freestyle.

When the paint dried it was ready for the rusty, hand made kiln. First she placed dry sheep manure on the ground, then to separate the new pottery from the manure she laid down some large, broken pot shards. On the shards she placed the pottery in a circular cluster, covered the sides with more large pot shards and placed an old car hubcap on top. Dried sheep manure then covered the entire pile. The old traditional pottery makers believe that a modern kiln "kills the spirit" of the pot. The sheep manure is then ignited and more fuel is added to the fire for several hours to complete the baking process. By the way, the sheep manure does not have an unpleasant odor, either before or during the burning process.

The interviews with Nellie Nampeyo were also very interesting. She related the reaction of her village the first time they were visited by an automobile. People of the village heard the noise for some time, but when the car appeared over a knoll they had no idea what it was. The bumper looked like the mouth of a giant creature, the headlights looked like eyes and the sight caused everyone to panic. The passengers of this first automobile were Mormon missionaries.

Nellie was a Tewa Indian and came from an exclusively Tewa village, within the Hopi reservation. The story of how this came to be is also very interesting. When the Spanish arrived in the New World they were centered in Mexico, but sent expeditions into what is now Arizona and New Mexico searching for Cibola, the city of gold. For fifty or more years they ruled over the native Americans in a ruthless manner. Finally, the native Americans had enough and there was an uprising that included the Tewa tribe from an area near Santa Fe, New Mexico.

I think it was fifty or seventy-five years later, word went out among the tribes that the Spanish Conquistadors were going to return and the Tewa Indians, fearing a harsh punishment for their part in the uprising, packed up and moved to the Hopi reservation for protection. The Hopi tribe gave the Tewa permission to establish a village within their territory and it has been there ever since in a friendly relationship. A fascinating thing is that at the time of my conversation with Nellie, the Tewa tribe had maintained their customs without being assimilated into the Hopi culture and there was very little, if any, intermarriage with outside ethnic groups. This is an example of just how fiercely native Americans guard and preserve their heritage.

CHAPTER VIII
ROCKY MOUNTAIN NATIONAL PARK
May 23, 1965 – November 1966

I was thrilled for the opportunity to work in Rocky Mountain National Park. The assignment was on the west side of the Park, but at that time the National Park Service also managed the adjoining Shadow Mountain National Recreation Area. The recreation area was composed of Grand Lake, which was a natural lake, plus two reservoirs known as Shadow Mountain Lake and Lake Granby. The picturesque little village of Grand Lake was nestled at the foot of the mountains and along the lakeshore. The town had a community building where movies were shown once a week during the summer months. I recall seeing our first 007 movie in this building. I joined the small Rotary Club of Grand Lake, with probably less than twenty members, and we had a most unusual meeting location. We met at the local bar, not in the back room but at the actual bar. This fact may account for why I have little memory of our community projects and meeting programs.

There were three new Park Service houses built a couple miles inside the Park adjacent to Trail Ridge Road, and we lived in quarters #461 paying rent of $29.00 bi-weekly. Most of the employees lived in houses of the old dam construction camp on Shadow Mountain Lake.

The Colorado River was once named the Grand River, hence the name of the lake, but the headwaters of the river is actually upstream in the adjacent Kawuneeche Valley of Rocky Mountain National Park, a sparkling clear, cold trout stream that one can jump across. There was a large tunnel constructed from Grand Lake under the Continental Divide, with an outlet on the east side of the mountains to divert water for cities on the east slope of the mountain. This tunnel was large enough that a Jeep Wrangler could be driven through it.

The Park was divided along the Continental Divide into east and west districts. It was about a fifty mile drive over Trail Ridge Road from the west side to Park headquarters and that road reached elevations over 12,000 feet. About half the year Trail Ridge Road was closed by snow, so the west side was even more isolated. Then the drive to headquarters over snow packed roads became by way of Granby, then U.S. Hwy 40 to

Idaho Springs and then north over a winding, narrow road to Estes Park, a distance of about 150 miles.

It was quite a new experience to live at 9,000 feet elevation in the Kawuneeche Valley on the west side of the Park, and this was the elevation of the valley floor. Water boils at a lower temperature at this elevation, so it was difficult to boil potatoes or make hot coffee. Some of the meal preparation had to be done in a pressure cooker. There were long months of deep snow, but we enjoyed the winter activities and if you didn't ski you were something of a social outcast, so the family all learned to ski at nearby Winter Park. Ski joring was also a popular activity between our house and Phantom Valley Ranch, several miles into the Park. Ski joring is something like water skiing behind a motorboat, but in this case a rope was tied to the bumper of the car and skiers held on the other end and skied on the road shoulders and ditches.

Kawuneeche Valley, Rocky Mountain National Park, Colorado

There was a small resort lodge located on a hillside above the village of Grand Lake, and near the lodge a small medical facility with a part time doctor and nurse that could handle minor medical needs and at least provide first aid until patients were moved to other facilities. In one unusual incident I transported a young boy to the facility who had been struck by lightening. The young lad was walking with his father and other companions from Shadow Mountain reservoir and passed near a metal gate at the time of a lightening strike. The bolt of lightening struck a metal fence, followed the wire fence to a metal gate and then jumped to the boy, knocking him to the ground unconscious. I responded to the emergency radio call and when placing the boy in the ambulance we administered resuscitation, but blood was running from his mouth and he appeared to be lifeless. I rushed him to the local medical facility and its doctor and nurse. When I checked back on him a couple hours later he had recovered and with no apparent ill effects, so that was a happy ending.

It was interesting to note the different preferences between visitors that came to Rocky Mountain National Park versus visitors that came to Shadow Mountain National Recreation Area. Park visitors usually remained for a longer time and preferred hiking, sightseeing, a wilderness experience and more privacy when camping. The campers at Shadow Mountain National Recreation Area did not visit the area for a wilderness experience but water recreation. The National Park Service had constructed nicely designed campgrounds, which were always filled to capacity on summer weekends. To accommodate the overflow we parked the pickup campers and house trailers side-by-side in the paved parking lots. We discovered that most campers were perfectly happy and actually had a preference for this high-density camping arrangement.

Johnny Holzworth owned a private dude ranch in the Park, several miles up the valley from our employee housing area. He was a short, bowlegged, crusty old guy and even in his seventies, he still did all the farrier work on his seventy plus horses. One time a crew from the electric company was relocating power poles and electric lines up the valley to make them less visible from the Park road, a project financed by the Park Service. Johnny got into a dispute with the power company foreman, a Mr. Gingery, and ran the crew off the job with a few shots from his hunting rifle. The terrified crew reported the incident to me. Fortunately, Mr. Holzworth and I had a good relationship and I negotiated a settlement, also advising Johnny that it was a serious crime, like assault with a deadly weapon, to even point a gun at people, and much more serious to shoot at people, even if you didn't intend to injure them. He accepted my warning and advice so that ended the problem with the power company.   As a point of interest, years later when I became Superintendent of Glacier National Park, Maurice Gingery was on the Park's maintenance staff and he was the brother of this Mr. Gingery of the power company in Colorado.

Rocky Mountain National Park, Colorado

There were only a few black bears in Rocky Mountain National Park but a fairly large male bear started hanging out along Trail Ridge Road begging for handouts from Park visitors. This situation has a high risk of injury to visitors feeding the bear and a screwed up diet for the bear, so we were looking for an opportunity to trap and move the animal. One day ranger Bert McLaren and I were patrolling Trail Ridge Road in my brand new Park station wagon. The vehicle also served as an ambulance so a Stokes litter and blankets were part of the vehicle equipment. A few miles after the road started gaining elevation we spotted the troublesome bear at a viewpoint, standing on the rock wall with his head in a trash barrel. This was a time before bear proof trash containers came into use.

We had a dart gun in the car and Bert got off a good shot, hitting the bear in the hind hip with the tranquilizing dart. The bear quickly retreated from the trash barrel and tried to reach the dart with his mouth while going in circles on the rock wall. Eventually the tranquilizer began to take effect, the bear lost balance, fell from the wall and rolled down the mountain like a big basketball. He came to rest in the trees about a hundred and fifty yards below the road.

We called on the Park radio for assistance from other rangers because now we had to somehow carry this bear back up the mountain and transport it to a bear trap. The nearest bear trap was at Phantom Valley Ranch a few miles down the road, at the bottom of the mountain. In the meantime Bert and I carried the stokes litter down to the bear. We were able to roll the sleeping bear onto his back into the litter. We had a good supply of rope so tied each leg of the critter to the metal frame. I also opened the bear's mouth, placed a stick in it and tied his mouth shut, so should the bear awake he couldn't snap at us. In retrospect I was pretty naive to think these bonds could really hold the bear should he regain full consciousness.

By this time help arrived on the scene and we proceeded to carry the bear up the steep mountain slope, but the bear was heavy and footing was difficult. As we neared the road we could see a crowd of visitors had congregated at the viewpoint watching our activity. I didn't want people to think we were abusing Park wildlife, so hoping to hide the evidence we covered the bear with the blanket that had been in the litter. The blanket didn't do much good in covering our patient, but I overheard a lady say, "Look at those nice rangers taking such good care of the bear."

We loaded the bear, still tied to the stokes litter, into the back of my new government patrol car and started down the mountain. As we were approaching Phantom Valley Ranch we could hear the bear awaking from sleep and I was concerned he might break the bonds and be loose in this car I was responsible for. How would I explain the destruction of my new government vehicle to the Chief Ranger and Superintendent? Fortunately we made it to the bear trap just in time and transferred the bear before he fully recovered from the tranquilizing drug.

In the fall of the year, a fairly large elk herd congregates in the Kawuneeche Valley near Phantom Ranch and they put on a great show. The big bull elk will fight, lock horns and compete for dominion over the group of cow elk. There is a lot of "bugling", a screeching sound or calling made by the bull elk to attract the females. We made whistles to imitate that sound, to bring the elk herd closer to the road. One night after watching this spectacle it was getting dark and we all departed for our homes. However, one person remained all alone and his car battery was dead. He started walking to the nearest residence, which was the Holzworth Ranch a few miles away. It was dead quiet and dark, very dark, with only the stars of the heavens for light. As he was walking briskly down the road he heard the ominous clop, clop, clop of elk hooves striking the road surface, following close behind him. He stopped from time to time trying to see where the elk was, but in the total darkness he could see nothing. When he stopped walking the elk also stopped. Apparently the lovesick bull elk had heard our bugling from the road and came over to investigate. Eventually, the stranded hiker reached the Holzworth Ranch without incidence.

The Kawuneeche Valley was not only beautiful but had a rich history, including the old mining camp of Lulu City, a couple of interesting dude ranches and the Grand Ditch. The Grand Ditch on the west side of the valley, located about halfway up the mountainside, was at least eight feet wide. Hundreds of Chinese laborers, or coolies, worked on this project in the early 1900s and they lived in four or five large camps, identified as camp #1, camp #2, #3 and so on, along the ditch. Water collected from all the streams flowing down the mountainside flowed north in the ditch to a point where it was dumped over the Continental Divide and into the

Poudre River on the east side of the Divide, to provide water to cities on the east slope of the mountains.

Rocky Mountain National Park had acquired a surplus Tucker Snow Cat from Grand Canyon National Park, so the maintenance supervisor Stu Dennett, ranger Bert McLaren and I drove a flatbed truck to Grand Canyon to pick up the machine. Our route of travel took us through Moab, Utah where we stopped to have lunch, and as we were walking back to the truck we ran into Roger Contor on the sidewalk. Roger was Assistant Superintendent of Canyonlands National Park and he knew Bert McLaren. Bert introduced Stu and me to Roger and we continued a pleasant conversation. As we began to walk away Roger turned to me and said, "By the way, we have just received your name to fill the vacant Chief Ranger position, so you might be thinking of your response."

This news was a shock to me and I didn't say anything to reveal my thoughts, but my immediate instinct was to decline the job offer. However, when returning home I discussed it with the family and considering the better school situation and other amenities, we accepted the offer. In retrospect that was one of the best decisions we ever made. We all learned to love Moab and the tour of duty was just about the most enjoyable time of our Park Service career.

CHAPTER IX
CANYONLANDS & ARCHES NATIONAL PARKS
November 20, 1966 – June 1968

Canyonlands National Park was a new Park and established only a couple of years earlier. I would be the second Chief of I&RM (Chief Ranger and Chief Naturalist) following Jim Randall, who had only been there less than two years. It was a large, major National Park and the challenge of working and planning the new development was an interesting opportunity.

Moab is the headquarters for the combined Canyonlands National Park, Arches National Park and Natural Bridges National Monument. Our first home, nestled against a sandstone cliff of Arches National Park, was government quarters #5 with attached garage. Rental rate was $43.00 biweekly plus utilities. About a year later we took out a Veterans Administration loan of $20,000.00 and purchased a home on San Juan Court, in the Stienville subdivision of Moab.

Delicate Arch, Arches National Park, Utah

The Mormon settlers who founded Moab selected the name from the Bible and it means "A place far away" and that is a fitting name for the town because when you are in Moab you are a long distance from nowhere. The scenic environment of Moab is exceptional. A cliff of beautiful red Navajo sandstone over a thousand feet in elevation forms the west side of the valley. The LaSalle Mountains rising more than 12,000 feet in elevation provide a spectacular view to the east and the Colorado River bisects the valley north of town. Water from the river spreads out below ground level to provide a water table of only a few feet below the surface and provides a weather moderating influence during the summer months, similar to that of a giant evaporative cooler. The winter months are very mild and short in length, so Moab is a very scenic and comfortable place to live, if you prefer an isolated location. There is a beautiful red rock area a few miles south of Moab that rivals the beauty of popular locations such as Sedona, Arizona.

The Three Gossips, Arches National Park, Utah

Rafting on the Colorado River was just beginning to emerge as a popular sport while I was a ranger at Grand Canyon, and the Park Administration, especially the Chief Ranger were very skeptical if this was an appropriate activity in a National Park. At that time there were only about three companies that traveled through the Grand Canyon once or twice a year. They were the Hatch Brothers, I think based in the town of Hatch, Utah, Nevelle's River Expeditions, I think based in Bluff, Utah, and Georgie

White based in Los Angeles.   By the time I was working at Canyonlands National Park there were about twelve river running companies that had formed an organization called the "Western River Guides Association". Some of the new ones were Western River Expeditions, owned by David and Betty MacKay of Salt Lake City, Ken Slight River Runners of Green River, Utah, and Doc Marston, based in California.   He ran the river in wooden boats similar to the ones used by Major John Wesley Powell, the first river runner.

Edward Abby, author of the best seller book "Desert Solitaire", worked as a seasonal Park ranger at Arches National Park, and while working in that capacity wrote another best selling book, "The Monkey Wrench Gang".   It wasn't hard to identify some of the local characters in the book and one of them was Ken Slight. The super villain in the book is a Mormon Bishop, J. Dudley Love, a self-righteous vigilante, who wages a holy war against a gang of environmental activists, the Monkey Wrench Gang.   I believe this true-to-life character was Dan Black from Monticello, Utah and a San Juan County Commissioner during the time we lived in Moab.   By today's political standards Mr. Black would be a hardcore Tea Party conservative.   He didn't have much use for National Parks because they restricted cattle grazing and mining activity within their boundaries.

During the 1950s through the 1970s, Moab was a busy potash mining, uranium prospecting and processing center. These activities transformed a sleepy, remote community into a rapidly expanding town.   Arches National Monument had existed for many years but attracted very little tourism because of its remote location. However, about two years prior to our move to Moab, Canyondands National Park was created but as yet had not gained much publicity.   Bates Wilson was Superintendent of Arches, at that time a National Monument, now a National Park, and he was also very influential in the creation of Canyonlands National Park. When Canyonlands was established it was clustered with Arches and Natural Bridges National Monuments, with the central office above the Post Office in Moab, and Mr. Wilson was Superintendent of the cluster.

Bates Wilson was a likeable, outgoing cowboy who loved to be outdoors and roam the backcountry of Grand County in his Jeep.   He definitely was not a spit and polish uniform guy sitting behind a big mahogany desk, but had an abhorrent attitude toward office duties and was a lousy paper pusher. Bates wasn't a very good manager either but he was an outstanding public relations person and widely known throughout Utah as Mr. Canyonlands. He couldn't write a compelling letter or coherent report, but he was very skillful on a personal basis. He could take a group of influential people on a Jeep trip into the backcountry, cook up a fabulous campfire dinner, have a few drinks and entertain with funny stories by the hour. He was the best at this type of public relations that I have ever known and it was a treasured experience to have worked for him.

The Needles, Canyonlands National Park, Utah

A master plan for the development of Canyonlands had been prepared, but it requires years for the funding cycle to evolve and no facilities had been constructed, except rustic campsites with no water or sewer. There were a few house trailers for the employees at the Needles District in the southern portion of the Park and two house trailers at the Island in the Sky District in the north. Roads in the Park were unimproved trails that had been established by uranium prospectors, oil exploration crews and ranchers. A road over Elephant Hill in the Needles District was challenging and not for the faint of heart. The hill was a solid mass of sandstone rock, called "slick rock" because it was generally barren of soil and vegetation. The trail could be negotiated with a four-wheel drive vehicle if you were careful not to high center the vehicle on a boulder. However, the trail on the more precipitous, almost sheer cliff of the west side had been blasted out by prospectors. It was just wide enough for a Jeep or International Scout vehicle but there wasn't space enough to make switchback turns, so you had to drive down one switchback and then back down the next one. This was quite intimidating because of the narrow, very steep terrain, no guard rails and fatal consequences if the vehicle went over the edge.

Canyonlands is a difficult Park to travel because it is bisected by both the Colorado and Green Rivers, which meet in the center of the Park. Furthermore, the Park is composed of hundreds of intertwining canyons forming a virtual maze of topography. Consequently, to reach a point five miles airline distance, one might travel twenty or more miles.

Pictographs, Canyonlands National Park, Utah

On the west side of the Park there is also a detached section called Horseshoe Canyon. This is a serene, beautiful little canyon resembling a miniature Zion National Park. It also contains the most interesting Indian pictographs I have ever seen. This panel extends for about a hundred feet, under an overhang along the base of the cliff, and the figures are tall, about eight feet in height, black, ghost-like images. Some of the figures look like they are wearing long robes and have something resembling a crown on their heads. There are literally thousands of Indian pictographs and petroglyphs in the Moab region, but nothing resembles these figures.

The road on the descent into Horseshoe Canyon has deep sand dunes at the bottom, which can be negotiated going downhill but impossible to return through as an uphill climb. The only option is to continue onward and exit to the east over a crude, narrow trail blasted out of the side of a rock cliff. At one point a short section of the road had collapsed and a rustic log bridge was attached to the side of the cliff. It looked old and crudely constructed – would it hold our vehicles? It was a long way down.

After Horseshoe Canyon we followed a trail along the Orange Cliffs on the west rim of Millard Canyon, a very deep tributary of the Green River. These landmarks are all within Glen Canyon National Recreation Area, which borders Canyonlands on the west and south sides. Near the southwest part of Canyonlands, also the border between Garfield and Wayne Counties, a Jeep trail known as the Flint Trail descends from the rim at 7,000 feet elevation, into a plateau called "Land of Standing Rocks" at 5,000 feet elevation. This trail terminates near a broad river bottom called Spanish Bottom and this elevation is about 4,000 feet. An interesting feature along this trail is at a point near the bottom where black, tar-like oil is seeping from the side of the cliff.

After exploring the inner canyons we climbed back to the canyon rim and continued south. The further south we went the better the quality of road. Eventually we came to Hite, a small development with a marina and limited visitor services at the head of Lake Powell. This place was also the junction with White Canyon Road and crossing over the Colorado River. White Canyon Road is now mostly a paved road between Mexican Hat and Hanksville, Utah.

Even from Hite it is a long trip back to Moab and along the way we passed Natural Bridges National Monument. As I recall this loop trip required three or four days to complete. Even today there are just hundreds and hundreds of square miles of pure, unspoiled wilderness in this area. I don't think there is such an extensive, untrammeled wilderness area like this in the lower forty-eight states and it is so unique that it's difficult to comprehend. However, the recent push to develop energy resources may have changed this area in recent years.

Chesler Park Area, Canyonlands National Park, Utah

River-running was getting to be a popular activity on the Colorado and Green Rivers, but the Park Service had no way to monitor what was going on along the rivers. In a few months I was able to purchase a jet boat to patrol the river, but in the meantime David McKay, owner of Western River Expeditions, offered me space on his raft to go with a group he was escorting down the Colorado River. This trip was scheduled for the spring of 1969 while the water was high and I would board the raft at Moab and disembark at Hite.

Each major rapid on the Colorado River is rated on a scale of 1 to 10, with 10 being the most difficult. A rapid rated 10 was considered impassible and dangerous even for expert boatmen. A stretch of river we would be floating through is named Cataract Canyon and in high water at least one of the rapids, called Big Drop, was rated near a degree 10. There was a huge bolder the size of a large vehicle lodged right in the center of the river, plus other debris on the downstream side of the boulder. This created a big drop in water level and a giant whirlpool with powerful suction.

Up to this point the river had been peaceful and we were floating gently along enjoying the sights. Then we came to a slight turn in the river and we couldn't see what was ahead, but we certainly could hear an ominous roar of rapids downstream. Our thirty-three foot raft was loaded heavily in the center with supplies, plus ten or a dozen people on board. I was sitting at the rear of the raft taking movies with the camera packed in a water proof bag.

A second boat in our party pulled ashore, above the rapids, to watch our progress and success or failure in negotiating the Big Drop. Since I was concentrating on filming this activity I was unaware of what was happening to the raft. We drifted too close to the huge bolder, which caused the raft to tip rather precariously and then we dropped off into the big hole below and the entire raft was carried under water. I felt this sudden surge of cold water strike me, causing me to take a deep breath. Now that we were all completely submerged, all I could see was murky water. I was disoriented and couldn't determine if I was upside down or what. Finally I needed to grab some air, so let go of the rope I was holding, dropped away from the raft and swam for the surface.

Everyone survived, but the raft suffered a large L-shaped rip about three feet long and eighteen inches in the other direction. It just happened that we had three medical students in our boat party and they were experienced in suturing injuries in people, so they proceeded to sew together the tear in our raft. This was covered with a waterproof paste and before long we were once again seaworthy.

CHAPTER X
DINOSAUR NATIONAL MONUMENT
June 1968 - April 1970

Once again the family was very content in Moab, which was a very livable town. We all had developed close friendships, the climate was moderate and it certainly was a scenic area, so we were not interested in moving just yet. However, when the job offer came for Superintendent of Dinosaur National Monument, it was difficult to decline the offer. In my estimation the job of Superintendent is the most coveted job in the National Park Service, the barrier to break into this rank is very competitive and the position is highly respected. The Superintendent is responsible for everything and everybody in the Park. I couldn't deny this opportunity that might never come my way again. Homes were pretty much assigned with the position on the staff and our modern, Mission 66 house was quarters #86, for which we paid rent of $36.00 biweekly.

Dinosaur is located in the states of Utah and Colorado, and the northern border is close to the state of Wyoming. The Park is in the shape of an inverted letter "T" and bisected by two large rivers, the Green entering the Park from the north and the Yampa entering the Park from the east. They converge at Echo Park, also known as Pat's Hole, near the center of the Park.

The Park has two distinct points of interest. The Quarry area has a large Visitor Center built over a cliff virtually covered with dinosaur bones, where visitors from the vantage point of an elevated walkway can observe technicians chipping away the rock to expose the dinosaur bones. The other major development is the Park headquarters located on U.S. Hwy 40 in the state of Colorado, just a few miles east of the Utah/Colorado border. This section has an attractive Administration/Visitor Center, Maintenance/Utility building, several houses and a couple of apartment buildings. This area is also the access to the rivers and Pat's Hole, or Echo Park.

Pat's Hole was named after Pat Lynch, a hermit and refugee from civilization. Mr. Lynch was born in Ireland and his real name was James Cooper. As a youth he obtained passage on a ship bound for Africa, but he was a hot-tempered youth who got into a fight with the ship's first mate and escaped punishment by jumping over the side of the ship and swimming over a mile to the African coast. There he joined a black tribe, married a black girl, had two sons and settled down for a few years. Tired of this life, he walked to the coast and secured passage on a ship bound for America. Was it a slave ship? I think he earned passage by working as a cook. He arrived in American just in time for the Civil War, enlisted in the Union Navy on a Mississippi gunboat and during battle he was wounded by a shell to his knee. After recovering, he joined the Union Army for the final year of the war.

Following his discharge from the Army, Pat obtained a job with a construction crew in St. Louis, Missouri where his hot temper again got him in trouble. In a disagreement with the crew foreman he struck the man in the head with a steel bar and thought he had killed him. He headed for the southwestern part of the United States, changed his name to Pat Lynch and enlisted in the U.S. Cavalry for three years. Following that assignment he came to Utah and settled into Pat's Hole, where he raised good quality Morgan horses and a few cattle. For the remainder of his life Pat stayed out of trouble and was a recluse, but known to be a very honest, independent man and a good neighbor.

Quarry Visitor Center, Dinosaur National Monument

Dinosaur was named for the widely known great deposits of dinosaur bones at the Quarry area. However, the Park has other very diverse attractions, including a rich history in the early settlers and wars between cattle and sheep ranchers, and some interesting archeological sites. A second generation of the Mantle family lived on a family ranch in a canyon of the Park and rumor was that the original livestock was acquired by rustling cattle from ranches in the neighboring states of Utah and Wyoming. A woman named Josie Morris had a ranch in Brown's Park in the western part of the Park near the Utah and Colorado border. Josephine, or Josie and her famous sister, Queen Ann were daughters of Herb Bassett, a prominent family respected by neighbors in Brown's Park. Both girls had a colorful past and knew all the early settlers and drifters, including Robert Leroy Parker, better known as Butch Cassidy. In the early days, Brown's Park had quite a few inhabitants and more than the average number of notorious outlaws. Josie's sister was known as Queen Ann the cattle Queen, and while we were living in the Park, Life Magazine ran a feature story on her.

Ann Bassett is described by author John Rolff Burroughs in his book "Where The Old West Stayed Young" as ". . . not merely good-looking; she was an extremely attractive lady. Arriving at maturity, she stood five feet three inches tall, weighed a hundred and fifteen pounds, possessed an 'hour glass' figure without the assistance of corsets, which, loathing them, she seldom wore, and had large, deceptively mild gray eyes and naturally wavy auburn hair. As spirited as she was high-strung, and highly intelligent (She had attended a girls school in Boston). Suiting her own convenience or caprice Ann could play the role of a cultured young gentlewoman, full to over flowing with gentility plus the innate Bassett charm; or she could be a perfect little hell-cat capable of throwing and breaking things, in command of a vocabulary that would cause a livery-stable hanger-on to blush with shame. Not only attractive, but resident in a piece of country where the ratio of males to females stood at six to one, Ann was tremendously popular, as indeed, was her older sister Josephine. The Bassett girls were, in fact, lodestones which attracted every unattached young man in Western Routt County to the eastern end of Brown's Park."

Queen Ann was arrested on charges of rustling Two Bar beef and author Burroughs reported the outcome of the first trial, "Queen Ann Sick In

Texas. It is doubtful if the case against Mrs. Ann Bassett Bernard will come up at this session, as word has been received that the defendant is ill in Texas." At the second trial in Craig, Colorado court, Ann was acquitted. Again Mr. Burroughs reports in his book, ". . . The outcome of the trial never for a moment was in doubt. That Ann was guilty as sin was beside the point. In her writings, Ann says, ' I did everything they ever accused me of, and a whole lot more.' Everybody knew it and very few people in Northwestern Colorado cared two hoots in a hollow. She was a heroine. She looked and acted the part. A lone woman, a smallish woman, a woman still young and exceedingly attractive had fought the mighty Haley (her accuser) to a standstill. Holding him up to public obloquy, Ann Bassett had whipped the daylights out of him." I think this last trial occurred in about 1915 or 1916. In 1920, Ann Bassett was still a fairly young lady and a widow. She married Frank Willis and they had a cattle ranch near Hackberry, Arizona near Kingman, then moved to Leeds, Utah where Frank worked for a gold mining company.

Ann died May, 1956 at the age of seventy-eight. My tenure at Dinosaur was 1968 through April 1970, so Queen Ann was fairly recent history at the time. Josie Bassett Morris had a small log cabin, still standing in Dinosaur National Monument when we lived there, and hopefully it is still standing.

I developed a friendship with Joe Haslem, who operated a cattle ranch adjoining the Park, and although getting along in years, he sat straight and proud in the saddle. He was a real genuine, hard working cattleman. Joe had lived in Utah all his life and most of it in the Dinosaur area. He knew all the old-timers such as Josie Morris and Pat Lynch. Joe said you had to be on good terms with your neighbors because many of them were cattle rustlers and if you were friends they wouldn't eat your beef. I recorded an interview with Joe for the Park's historical files and he commented on what a slovenly person Pat Lynch was. He never took a bath and one time when he had guests they washed their hands before having a meal. Pat picked up the washbasin and drank the water, much to the disgust and astonishment of his company. When Pat saw their expression he commented something like, "Well, what won't kill you will feed you."

There must have been a concentration of rustlers living in the Brown's

Park and Diamond Mountain areas as noted by a newcomer to the area. Brown's Park is the area along the Green River in Utah and Colorado and Diamond Mountain is a plateau north of that. The outlaw Matt Warner – his real name was Willard Christensen – had left home (in Denmark ?) from necessity at the age of thirteen. He went to work for Jim Warren in 1878 and he has the following comment regarding the Diamond Mountain ranching operation of that day, "I hadn't worked for Jim Warren for a week till I knew that in running away from the law, I had run smack into the half-outlaw world. Diamond Mountain was a half-outlaw world because the ranchers there made their living partly by regular ranch business and partly by rustling. Every outfit but one, an Eastern horse breeding outfit rustled whenever it had a chance to do it secretly and safely."

One of our rangers, Barry Ashworth, lived and worked in the Thousand Island area, in the western part of Dinosaur National Monument. He was walking his dog along the boundary of the Park when the dog stopped to sniff an odd shaped object sticking out of the ground. Fortunately, Barry restrained the dog because this object was a cyanide gun used to kill coyotes. The object sticking out of the ground was similar in appearance and size to a large cigar, but it was a lethal bait used to attract the animal. When the coyote, or pet dog, pulled at the bait it triggers a projectile which shoots cyanide into the mouth and throat, killing the animal. These killing devices were known as 1080 bait stations and the trappers were required to mark the location with posts painted red on top. Unfortunately, dogs, marmots, badgers, prairie dogs and other animals can't read these signs and many were killed along with the coyotes. Barry almost lost his dog.

I was infuriated when ranger Ashworth reported this incident. This bait station on the border of the Park was established by the predator control unit of the U.S. Fish and Wildlife Service, a sister agency of the National Park Service within the U.S. Department of the Interior. Since the two agencies within the same Department of the Interior had opposite objectives toward wildlife, they had an interagency agreement that no 1080 stations would be located within, as I remember, two miles of a National Park's exterior boundary. This bait station was a violation of that agreement and was also located near several homes, extremely hazardous to children and pets living in the area. I think it was the stupidity of the person who established this bait station that infuriated me the most. I told the U.S. Fish and Wildlife Service in brutal language to abolish that bait station and they sheepishly apologized.

This incident had strong repercussions with the large number of sheep ranchers in the area, because they had the impression that the Park was a breeding ground for all the coyotes in the area and in their opinion the only good coyote was a dead coyote. A lot of these sheep ranchers had a bumper sticker on their pickup trucks that said, "Eat Lamb, 10,000 Coyotes Can't Be Wrong". The sheep ranching business was a significant part of the local economy and so this confrontation received a lot of fuss in the news media and I had a considerable public relations problem to deal with. Coinciding with all of this, the Sheep Ranchers Association was having an annual meeting in nearby Craig, Colorado and invited me to speak to the group, no doubt looking forward to having me for a gang bang roast.

I was not looking forward to such an affair, but my philosophy is, if you have a problem it must be dealt with and resolved, the sooner the better or it will grow more contentious, so I agreed to attend the meeting. Joe Haslem, my friend and local cattle rancher heard of my invitation and offered to go with me because he knew many of these sheep ranchers. I guess Joe felt that maybe he could bridge some of the gap in relationship to this group that I didn't know, and I felt a deep appreciation for his kindness to me.

It was about an hour and a half drive to Craig, so Joe and I left early to allow for any delay and be at the meeting on time. We arrived early but there was already a large crowd of sheep ranchers in the bar and we exchanged a few drinks with the group. In fact, by the time the meeting began everyone was pretty mellow. My explanation to the ranchers about the problem with the bait station went across better than expected and this public relations problem was resolved more successfully than I could have ever hoped, thanks in great part to my friend Joe Haslem.

We were living at Dinosaur during the centennial of the John Wesley Powell expedition down the Colorado and Green Rivers. This was even more eventful for us because my wife's family, the Swains, were distant relatives of the Powell family, through Mr. Powell's sister. Also, Mr.

Powell had taught school in Hennepin, Illinois during his younger years. Hennepin is a picturesque small village, on the east bank of the Illinois River, and the county seat for Putnam County, which includes McNabb, Illinois, Patricia's hometown. Patricia was honored by unveiling a new plaque dedicated to John Wesley Powell.

Fossils at Dinosaur National Monument

During my tenure at Dinosaur, nearby Flaming Gorge National Recreation area was being transferred to the U.S. Forest Service, so during this transition I was also appointed as Superintendent of Flaming Gorge. Also, in addition to that new responsibility, I was designated as "Keyman" for the proposed Fossil Butte National Monument near Kemmerer, Wyoming. The responsibility of a Keyman was to work with the local citizens in the vicinity of the proposed Park area to determine if they wanted the new Park and if so, to help them through the process of creation.

Proponents of the Park had a loosely affiliated organization headed by a dairy farmer west of Kemmerer, but the local businessmen were intimidated by people in the area opposing establishment of the Park. They threatened to boycott any business that supported the Park idea and businessmen in this little town were struggling to survive. As a note of interest, Kemmerer, Wyoming was the home of J. C. Penney and his first store was still in business, maintained in the original appearance. The store originally operated under the name of "The Golden Rule" which is, "Do unto others as you would have others do unto you." Mr. Penney was a devout Christian and required his employees to attend church on Sunday. Times have changed.

Don Kominsky, editor of the Kemmerer Gazette, and the Ulrich family, who operated a fossil quarry in the area, were strong proponents of the Park and became close personal friends. On April 16, 1969 I had a phone call from John Kawamoto, legislative liaison in the National Park Service Regional Office, to bring me up to date on progress to establish the Park. Congressman Wold sponsored the legislation and was persuaded to consider opinions other than those of the ranchers. In fact, the National Park Service was going to draft a bill for the Congressman, but this was strictly confidential and the information could not be divulged to anyone. I had the pleasure of going to Washington, DC for the Senate hearings, the Park was established, and the experience was a very rewarding one. I was also invited to join Senator Cliff Hanson for lunch in the Senate dining room. I recall that on a certain day of the week it was a custom, no actually an act of Congress, to serve bean soup in the Senate dining room every Friday. I guess this was a law sponsored by the Senator from Maine.

CHAPTER XI
MIDWEST REGIONAL OFFICE
OMAHA, NEBRASKA
April 1970 - June 1972

At this time in history, the National Park Service Midwest Regional Office in Omaha, NE covered the largest region in the agency and included ten states, from Iowa to Montana and south to southern Utah. The region also included many of the largest National Parks, such as Yellowstone, Grand Teton, Rocky Mountain and Glacier National Park.

The Washington Office had just issued a mandate that all Park superintendents should have prerequisite experience in a central office, i.e. Washington office or one of the Regional Offices. To fulfill that requirement I was transferred to the Midwest Regional Office in Omaha as Assistant Regional Director. The larger National Parks are staffed with a broad range of specialists but the smaller parks and monuments were not, so my division of the Regional Office provided that support as needed. My division filled the entire third floor of the Regional Office and included Concession Management, Land Acquisition, Ranger Activities, Law Enforcement, Interpretation, Maintenance, Architecture, Landscape Architecture and Historic Architecture. Some of these units had a sizeable staff, but if we didn't have the particular expertise needed for the task I could also borrow such talent from one of the larger Parks.

A significant part of my time was involved with the numerous Indian tribes that adjoined many of the National Park areas and this was a time of turmoil and demonstrations by some of the younger members of the tribes. For example, on June 6, 1971 Clyde Bellecourt and Russell Means announced that they intended to take possession of Mount Rushmore National Monument and on that day Superintendent Wally McCaw phoned to tell me that forty or fifty Indians had invaded the Park armed with clubs, baseball bats and pick axe handles.

We had made preparations by dispatching rangers from other Parks, officers from the National Capitol Park Police (a branch of the National Park Service), South Dakota National Guard, Bennington and Custer County Sheriffs Dept., South Dakota Highway Patrol, South Dakota State Game and Fish Dept., U.S. Marshall Service, U.S. Attorney and the FBI. We had over eighty law enforcement personnel assembled and regained control of Mount Rushmore in short order. This type of major encounter of course attracted a lot of media attention, so we provided constant briefing to all political persons, all the way up to the White House. As usual there were a few armchair second guessers on the handling of this affair, but it was an excellent production and about a week later, in Rapid City, SD, our adversary Russell Means stated that the National Park Service did a good job in handling this affair.

George Hartzog was Director of the National Park Service at this time and he was a very active, dynamic and strong leader. He was also a skillful politician and as a result, the National Park Service came to the forefront of attention among many political leaders. The organization lost much of its innocence during this time, but did prosper by a rapid expansion of new Park areas and the development of new facilities.

George was an outgoing personality and seemed to meet many interesting people during his travels. He hired some of them on the spot, much to the dismay of folks in the personnel department who had to juggle positions and write position descriptions to support the high-grade level of these new people. One of the interesting people hired by George was a former U.S. Congressman from South Dakota, Mr. Ben Rifle. Mr. Rifle's ethnic background was half German descent and half Sioux Indian. He was also very intelligent and a Rhodes scholar.

As mentioned previously, during this time there was a great deal of unrest among the younger members of several Indian tribes and some of the National Parks were staging grounds for demonstrations, Mount Rushmore in particular. The Indians were indignant that their sacred mountain had been desecrated with sculpture carvings of white man's presidents. Russell Means was one of the most prominent Indian leaders and he received a lot of money and support from some unknown sources and traveled all over the United States leading demonstrations.

Congressman Ben Rifle publicly reprimanded Mr. Means for his loud and noisy behavior, which as an elder of the Sioux tribe he felt was undignified and repugnant to proud elders of the tribe. Mr. Means retaliated by attacking Mr. Rifle as an Indian who was red on the outside but white on the inside. Russell concluded his remarks by challenging

Ben Rifle to a public debate. Mr. Rifle pulled himself up straight and tall and responded, "Yes, I will debate you, on one condition, and that is that the debate will be in the Sioux language." Those who witnessed this confrontation say that they could observe Mr. Means physically shrink in size because he had no response. He could not speak the Sioux language of his native tribe.

Mr. Rifle spoke at a Midwest Regional Superintendents conference and certainly made an impression on me. His purpose was to provide us with an insight into the Indian culture, behavior and thinking. Indians were always late for meetings and this was commonly referred to as "Indian Time", which meant Indians had no concept of time, or had little regard for the need of punctuality. Another cultural conflict was the Indians', or native Americans', disregard for advance planning or the need to show up for work if something more interesting was going on with the tribe.

Mr. Rifle pointed out that since the beginning of time, until recently, Indian people lived off the land. They moved about with the grazing buffalo and gathered food when plants were in season. Even if they did have surplus food they did not have the opportunity to preserve it, except during winter months. Therefore, there was not a need for planning or keeping a schedule. The people had to adapt to whatever Mother Nature offered at the present time. As a matter of survival the people also had to share the food with other members of the tribe who were less fortunate. As a result of doing this for centuries, many of them had not yet adapted to the white man's culture of putting aside money and other possessions for a future need. It may take four or five generations for these patterns of thinking to change.

A later experience brought this cultural difference to mind. As Assistant Regional Director (title escalation later changed the title to Associate Regional Director), one of my responsibilities was the oversight of Park concessions, including the issuance of contracts to operate within a Park. My division chief was John Spurgeon, who was a lawyer and his primary function was handling the legal aspects of a concession contract. The Sioux Indians were pushing the National Park Service to award them some of the lucrative concession operations, and in particular the Mount Rushmore operation. Kay Burgess Riordon and her nephew Jack Riordon operated the Mount Rushmore facility and did a very good job of it.

This was one of the best concession operations in all of the National Parks and the Indians wanted to take over the operation. Being aware of the Indians' inexperience with such business operations, it would be a great disservice to Kay Burgess, Park visitors and the tribe to take over such an operation at top performance. Fortunately, about the same time another nearby concession contract was going to be available at Badlands National Monument. This was a small, but good little operation that would give the Indians an opportunity to gain experience on a smaller scale and we awarded the contract to them.

The management and employees of the business were all members of the Sioux tribe and it didn't take long before it was evident the business was floundering. If there was a special Indian dance on the reservation many of the employees would not come to work. If a member of the tribe was in need of money it was taken from the cash register. This person did not consider taking money from the cash register as stealing – he just regarded this money as community property. When it came to ordering inventory to restock the shelves it was not accomplished. This was not a lack of intelligence. No, they were following cultural custom of living day by day and the concept of planning ahead was still foreign to them. Fortunately, the Indians also realized their problem and hired a white man with business experience to manage the business.

While working in the Regional Office I was occasionally called upon to participated in field reviews with an evaluation team. Bob Giles, the Regional Administrative Officer, was the permanent head of this team and he would select two other people from the office to participate as temporary members of the team. We would travel to a Park and usually spend three to five days reviewing the Park operation, maintenance and management. Each member of the team made a broad overview but concentrated on that part of management within their area of expertise and experience. The object of the review was to look for facets of the operation that could be improved, but also recognize aspects that were exceptionally successful, to identify problems that needed assistance from the Regional Office and assure compliance with regulations and accounting procedures. At the conclusion of our work we met with the Superintendent and other staff members to review our report and solicit their comments. This was an excellent, productive program and Bob Giles was the ideal team leader and diplomatic contact with the Park staff.

On one of these evaluation review trips Bob Giles, Pat Miller and myself visited Custer Battlefield, the Park now renamed as Big Hole Battlefield National Historic Park. Randy Pope was the Superintendent, a former historian and now a very good Superintendent. It was obvious that Randy had a bright future in the National Park Service. This is an interesting Park, with an active National Military Cemetery, a good interpretive center and of course was the scene of a great historic battle, won this time by the Native Americans.

The Indians were defending their territory against an arrogant and egotistical George Armstrong Custer, commander of the 7th Cavalry. Custer had made a name for himself during the Civil War. Maybe this hero worship distorted his sense of reality. The defeat and death of the troops was totally unnecessary and would not have happened if Custer had followed orders and withheld confrontation until other troops that were scheduled to arrive the next day showed up, but Custer didn't want to share the glory of defeating the Indians in battle.

After Custer and the 7th Cavalry were annihilated, General Custer again became a national hero, thanks to the efforts of his influential wife, Libby. She bombarded the news media with letters, books and newspaper interviews to immortalize her husband. The basement of the administrative building at the battlefield contained many of Mr. and Mrs. Custer's personal possessions, filing cabinets full of letters and correspondence, the General's buckskin clothing, boots, saddle, shaving brush, tooth brush, even his jock strap, on and on. This was a great resource for historians and General Custer buffs. Superintendent Pope said some of the more ardent admirers, when visiting this room in the basement, actually fell into a trance, enraptured by the presence of these very personal belongings of Mr. Custer. Randy said some of these people were so entranced that they would be oblivious to anything going on around them.

It was fitting and proper to change the name of this historic battlefield because when it was called Custer Battlefield, it had almost become a shrine to Custer. The historic presentation of the battle was not complete and was distorted. The battle took place on June 25th and on that date each year, Park employees would find flowers at Custer's memorial at the top of the hill, honoring him. Up until that time no one had seen the person or persons who were honoring General Custer.   However, they did occasionally see visitors kneeling at this location as if in deep reverence or prayer on behalf of, or to, the spirit of George Armstrong Custer.   Little has changed over the years at the battlefield site and area surrounding the Park, so one can really visualize the battle scene just as it was about one hundred and fifty years ago.

CHAPTER XII
UTAH STATE DIRECTOR
SALT LAKE CITY, UTAH
June 1972 – February 1974

George W. Hartzog, Director of the National Park Service, was a great innovator and experimenter. During his era it seemed that the National Park Service was frequently reorganizing the structure of our agency. One of his ideas was to establish an office of State Director in four states where the National Park Service had a high profile such as Utah, Arizona, Colorado and Hawaii (which included a cluster of all National Park Service areas in the Pacific). I was assigned to the state of Utah, which had more land dedicated to National Park areas than any other state. More land has been added since that time but as I recall, at this time about five percent of the state was National Park area.

There was no precedence for this organizational structure, no instruction from the Washington office or job description, so we felt our way along and designed our duties as we thought productive to our agency and the state. This was a time when Environmental Impact Statements evolved and this resulted in closer relationships with other state and federal agencies. Our office was in the Federal Building in downtown Salt Lake City and I had an excellent assistant Jim Isenogle. We divided the work so that Jim concentrated his efforts working with Utah State agencies, such as the Utah Department of Natural Resources, State Parks, etc. I concentrated my attention to other federal agencies such as the U.S. Forest Service, Bureau of Land Management, U.S. Attorney and United States Solicitor. Incidentally, the U.S. Solicitor was Tom Parker, a distant relative of another Parker better known as Billy the Kid. We also operated a small information office.

The working arrangement between Jim Isnogle and myself turned out to be very productive and this assignment proved to be one of the most rewarding work experiences of my career. For many years Bob Nielson, State Director of the Bureau of Land Management, was very antagonistic toward the National Park Service because of a bad public relations incident with a Park Superintendent many years ago. Whenever a National Park boundary was adjusted, enlarged or a new Park created, it involved an exchange of government land. That land usually came from the Bureau of Land Management. Of course the Bureau of Land Management had nothing to gain from this land exchange and when the BLM State Director had a grudge against the NPS, such an exchange became much more difficult if not impossible.

Bob Nielson and I became very good friends and from that time on land exchanges were handled very efficiently, and that alone made the state office in Utah a worthwhile experiment. Another significant incident occurred at Glen Canyon National Recreation Area, on the boundary between Utah and Arizona. The Recreation Area was a fairly new creation and experiencing a lot of development. Governor Calvin Rampton of Utah was upset with the National Park Service because he didn't think the State of Utah had been involved enough in the master plan for the area. Consequently, he issued an executive order establishing an "Advisory Council" for the future planning and development of Glen Canyon. I liked Governor Rampton and he was a good supporter of the National Parks, but this was a delicate situation because we didn't want to inject another bureaucratic level of management into the operation, but we also wanted to appease the Governor's concerns. I had a meeting with Lee Kapalowski of the State Planning Office, and Bill Bruhn and Gordon Harmston with the State Dept. of Natural Resources. Together we diplomatically resolved the Governor's concerns by an understanding that this was to be a short-term committee.

There were several National Park employees scattered about the state of Utah, most of them working on special statewide research projects. The Regional Office was at a loss for what to do with them, so dumped all of them under my supervision. They required very little attention from me and this arrangement worked out just fine. One of the employees was of special interest to me. He was a biologist attached to Professor Thadis W. Box, Dean of the College of Natural Resources, Utah State University at Logan, Utah. This arrangement was something of an accident but I could see great potential for opportunities in other states. This placed a National Park Service employee as a liaison connecting college graduate students looking for research projects, with the Parks needing research in any number of fields. A big mutual benefit.

At this time river running activity on the Colorado and Green Rivers was experiencing explosive growth and it was apparent to all state and federal agencies that there needed to be some guidelines and control to protect the river environment and a quality visitor experience. I knew all of these river guides and companies from my tours of operation at Grand Canyon, Canyonlands and Dinosaur National Parks. About a dozen river running companies existed and they had organized the Western River Guides Association. I believe Jack Currey or Dave McKay of Salt Lake City was the first president. Within a few years well over a hundred people were attending these meetings and they were no longer informal, intimate gatherings.

The Federal Court in Salt Lake City was just down the street from the Federal Building and the eccentric judge was Mr. Ritter. He was a short, rotund little man and ran his office and surroundings like a little kingdom. Fortunately, from my point of interest, Mr. Ritter was very partial to environmental issues and frequently issued some rather biased decisions. One time Judge Ritter made a decision that the waters of Lake Powell could not inundate the lands of adjacent Rainbow Bridge National Monument. This decision, like many others, was overturned by the Tenth Circuit Court of Appeals.

One day I was visiting Judge Ritter's courtroom because the case had something to do with Capitol Reef National Park. Judge Ritter spotted me in the room during the trial and without any advance notice, called me up to the stand as a witness. The young attorney in this case came from Washington, DC and was actually acting a bit arrogant as the big shot lawyer in this town of country hicks. Judge Ritter took an instant dislike to the young man and picked on him mercilessly. The lawyer didn't seem to accept his position as an officer of Judge Ritter's court and finally the short-tempered Judge jerked him to attention by accusing him with contempt of court and a threat of jail. I have never seen a person's disposition change so dramatically. He was deeply shaken, his complexion faded to an ashen gray color and he suddenly realized that he was on the verge of going to jail, perhaps ruining his legal career.

On another occasion Judge Ritter's courtroom proceedings were disturbed by the noise of city street workers repairing State Street at the front of his courtroom, Judge Ritter sent the bailiff out to the street crew with an order to stop working or face contempt of court. Life was always a circus around Judge Ritter.

Ron Walker was Director of the National Park Service during this time and his claim to fame was travel coordinator for President Nixon. Consequently, when Mr. Walker visited a National Park function he made travel arrangements as he would have for the President. He always provided a detailed travel itinerary like, "arrival at city airport, 7:53 pm, pick up baggage at 8:06 pm, depart in limousine at 8:16 pm, arrival at hotel at 8:43 pm etc. and he made a great fuss about maintaining these time schedules. However, Mr. Walker didn't know anything about the history, purpose or operation of the National Park Service. Consequently he made a lot of mistakes and wasted directives, but eventually he settled into the job and developed a respectful attitude toward the agency and employees.

President Nixon's staff people were a strange collection of people, very close knit, secretive, defensive, aloof and strangely, they all used a lot of profanity, sort of a juvenile illusion of macho, male virility. I had an occasion to deal with some of the White House staff at Glen Canyon National Recreation Area. The issue was concession policies and it certainly was a strange experience. Their attitude was to leave the concessioners alone, let them run their business as they saw fit, despite the fact they had a monopoly within a Park. After that experience I lost a lot of respect for President Nixon and his clan in the White House.

Living in Salt Lake City was an interesting and enjoyable experience. The Salt Lake Valley is a scenic location surrounded by the beautiful mountains and bordered by the Great Salt Lake. World-class ski areas, the Mormon history, historic Temple Square, the famous Mormon choir and all the countless scenic areas within the state made this a great place to live. Crime rate at this time was low, and an acquaintance in the FBI told me that organized crime didn't have an opportunity to establish a base of operation because of the strong control over virtually every aspect of life and commerce by the Mormon Church.

CHAPTER XIII
GLACIER NATIONAL PARK
FEBRUARY 1974 – SEPTEMBER 1980

During my tenure as Utah State Director I had been closely involved in the affairs of Glen Canyon National Recreation Area. Superintendent Corky Johnson had announced his plans for retirement and Regional Director Len Volz had indicated that he would like to have me succeed him as Superintendent. This was a lateral transfer but a tempting offer because in my estimation the job of Park Superintendent was the most desirable job in the National Park Service.

Based on Regional Director Len Volz's remarks, I had mentally placed our next family move to Page, Arizona. One day Mr. Volz did phone me with a job offer, but much to my surprise it was a job offer of Superintendent of Glacier National Park in Montana. The Montana Congressional delegation had already received the customary courtesy notice of my assignment. This was not only a promotion, a higher-ranking position than Glen Canyon, but Glacier National Park is one of the most coveted assignments in the National Park Service. Len explained that this job offer was issued from Park Headquarters in Washington DC and of course took precedence over his plans to move me to Glen Canyon. I would have been quite content with the job at Glen Canyon, but was beside myself with joy, absolutely thrilled with the perfect move to Glacier National Park. To this day I don't know who made this assignment change. It had to be the National Park Service Director or someone close to the Director, but I have never discovered the answer to that question.

The Superintendent's house in Glacier was a great and memorable living experience. It is an old two-story log house on the bank of the Middle Fork of the Flathead River, rustic but also charming and surrounded by a forest of beautiful, large conifer trees – douglas fir, white pine, ponderosa, larch and aspen. There was snow on the ground when we arrived but the temperature was rather mild. The most pronounced first impression to the senses was the fresh, crisp, clean air of Glacier National Park. It is indescribable. During my tour of duty at Glacier I traveled out of state quite often, but every time upon my return my heart would sing as I enjoyed the fragrant fresh air of northwest Montana.

Another thing about Glacier National Park that intrigued me was that it was also part of an International Peace Park, Waterton-Glacier International Peace Park established in 1932. The Peace Park idea was created by the Rotary Clubs of Montana and Alberta, Canada. It is an amazing accomplishment that the Rotary Clubs pushed this legislation through their respective national governments in less than one year. Now, each year the Rotarians from Alberta and Montana meet for a weekend to celebrate the existing peace between the two countries. The concept of an international peace park has expanded to many locations all over the world. A couple of years ago I was able to have the name of Chief Mountain Road changed to Chief Mountain International Peace Parkway, to further emphasize the connection between the two Parks.

The former Superintendent, Bill Briggle and I overlapped for two or three weeks to give me more familiarity with Park operations and significant issues on the scene. On the last day, as Briggle was leaving the scene, he casually mentioned, "Oh, I almost forgot to tell you that a couple of months ago (during the off season winter months) I closed Going-to-the-Sun Road to the use of bicycles. This use on such a narrow road is just incompatible with the heavy automobile traffic." My first thought was, who in their right mind would want to ride a bicycle on such a steeply elevated road anyway.

Well, as the summer season approached I began to receive more and more protests from bikers wanting to ride on the road. It was becoming apparent that this restriction on the road was controversial. I could not locate an organized group of bikers to talk to, so I contacted Jim Lecander who owned a bicycle store in Kalispell. He rounded up a couple of other bikers, came to the Park and we discussed the problem and possible solutions. I offered a compromise that bikers could ride Going-to-the-Sun Road during early hours of the day, prior to times of heavy traffic. This satisfied their need and I believe this plan is still in effect.

Glacier National Park had a history of significant issues that would pop up from time to time, such as grizzly bear attacks on Park visitors, raging forest fires, traffic congestion, visitor use management, land acquisition issues and environmental issues. However, by far the most controversial and significant decision I made was snowmobile use in the

Park. Superintendent John Townsley of Yellowstone National Park had encouraged snowmobile use in Yellowstone. The use rapidly expanded and became a huge economic impact in the area, so much so that the Park lost control on the extent of use.

Spring Opening, Going-to-the-Sun Road, Glacier N. P.

I didn't have negative feelings about snowmobile use but recalled in early summer months at Rocky Mountain National Park where snowmobile trails outside the Park were clearly evident in the meadow grass. The compacted snow of the trails allowed cold temperatures to penetrate deeper into the ground and kill the grass, so there was reason to believe that the machines might have an effect on the environment. Also, in narrow valleys of Glacier National Park, the noise of the machines created some stress on animals causing them to move away from the roadways, which were their frequent route of travel and forced their moves to the deep snow and more difficult travel routes.

There really was not a lot of snowmobiling activity going on in the Park. We were concerned mostly with activity along Lake McDonald and what it was doing to wildlife. There were moose and other animals drifting around in the wintertime in the valley. So we decided to prepare an environment impact statement, a process that had recently become a requirement for such issues.

Saint Mary's Lake, Glacier National Park, Montana

The impact statement contained several options and one of them was the elimination of snowmobile use altogether. Orin Blaken, a newscaster of local radio station KOFI was an ardent snowmobiler, and in fact, an officer in the Flathead Snowmobile Association.   He gave the subject a lot of publicity and stirred up the people who were proponents of snowmobile use.   This in turn aroused the Montana Wilderness Association and people opposed to snowmobile use in the Park, so the issue became a big controversial topic in western Montana

This was the first time Glacier had held public meetings outside the Park and we held a hearing in Great Falls and Kalispell. The hearing in Kalispell was a surprise. The same night of our public hearing at the Elks Lodge, the City of Kalispell was holding a controversial hearing on a new sewer treatment plant, which was a big issue in town and I was concerned it would draw most of the public away from our hearing. Well, our meeting was a standing room crowd of over five hundred people, including representatives from the Montana congressional delegation.   In contrast, the city hearing only had seventeen people in attendance and most of them were news media reporters.   I had not yet expressed my feelings on the issue and already Herb Sammons, one of the proponents from Cut Bank, Montana purchased a full page ad in the Hungry Horse News with three words, "Iversen Must Go".

After the public hearings I appointed a committee of equal numbers of proponents and opponents, to review all comments and give me their report.   This committee worked well together and in their discussion I think each side gained some understanding of the other side's concerns. In my final review I felt that we should consider the opportunity for snowmobile use throughout the area, on all public lands, BLM, U.S. Forest Service, State owned land and National Park Service. It was not necessary that each public agency had to accommodate all types of recreational activity, especially if adequate opportunities already existed. We must also consider the opportunity for cross country skiers to have quiet trails and animals to move about in their normal habitat without interruption. I had a Park staff meeting following the public hearings and asked input from each employee present.

It was apparent that the snowmobilers had abundant areas for recreation so I made the decision to exclude that activity in the Park. However, the snowmobile enthusiasts were convinced that they could overturn my decision and I was told that they had the financial resources to accomplish their objective. The Montana Snowmobile Association had a big annual meeting at the Fairmont Hot Springs resort near the town of Anaconda. They invited me to that meeting along with Superintendent John Townsley of Yellowstone National Park. John was their hero for encouraging snowmobile use at Yellowstone and I was their nemesis. It has always been my philosophy to face adversity head on rather than ignore it in the hope it will go away, so I accepted the invitation and made my presentation. I think the group respected me for coming to their meeting. They treated me with courtesy but probably didn't accept my talk with great enthusiasm. John Townsley also gave a talk and supported me by explaining the different circumstances between Glacier and Yellowstone. I felt that the meeting had been productive and the issue diminished a little. It was a good decision for the Park and after thirty plus years it may have been the most important decision I ever made on behalf of a National Park.

Lake McDonald, Glacier National Park, Montana

During the 1970s, kokanee salmon were an abundant fish species in rivers and lakes of the Flathead Valley. In the fall, the fish would swim upstream to spawn by the thousands and one active location was just below the outflow of McDonald Creek from Lake McDonald. After spawning, the fish would die and become an abundant food source for bald eagles, bear, coyotes and other wildlife. This wildlife display also became a popular event for people to observe. The Park made daily counts of the bald eagles because they were an endangered species and the number of eagles, as I recall, could be over four hundred at one time.

The eagles would swoop over McDonald Creek and pluck fish out of the water with their talons, then roost on a nearby tree branch to enjoy the feast. Unfortunately, in the late 1980s Fish and Game, in a plan to improve food sources for kokanee salmon, introduced a competitive species and destroyed habitat for the kokanee salmon and the fishery died out. An excerpt from my daily diary: Oct. 31, 1979 Bald eagle count along lower McDonald Creek total 287 with 132 mature eagles and 155 immature. Nov. 21, 1979 Bald eagle count on lower McDonald Creek 445 total with 297 mature and 148 immature eagles. Nov. 29, 1979 Bald eagle count along lower McDonald creek was 328 mature bald eagles and 139 immature eagles.

As I began my tenure at Glacier National Park there were still several hundred acres of private land holdings within the Park, which we referred to as "inholdings". We didn't make an effort to purchase these lands unless the owners wished to sell and it was made known that the government was always receptive to purchase. Then a bill was passed in Congress known as the Land and Water Conservation Act, which provided funding for State and Federal government agencies to purchase land. Money was taken from the lease of offshore oil drilling and used to fund the Land and Water Conservation Fund, so suddenly the National Park Service had money to purchase inholdings in the Park. Land acquisition people were hired to staff positions in Washington DC, the regional offices and even in some Parks, including Glacier. A capable man named Bob Lunger was assigned to Glacier and he initiated a very aggressive program by personally contacting every landowner to determine their interest in selling. Mr. Lunger purchased more land within a couple of years than all the years since and many years prior to his presence. Most of the sales were "Life Tenure" purchase agreements and this was a contract wherein the government purchased the property but the seller had a right to continue full use of the land until they died, then the transfer of land ownership actually took place. This was a very popular and successful program with all parties. Of the several hundred acres of inholdings that had existed, more than half of that land was acquired by the National Park Service.

When an inholder wanted to make a change in the existing use of their land, such as remodel or build a new structure, they were required to obtain Park approval because it could have an adverse impact on the Park environment and the law creating the Park. We only had one adverse and unpleasant land acquisition experience. A couple owned a lot at Kelly Camp, located across Lake McDonald from Lake McDonald Lodge. This Kelly Camp couple brought plans to me for the construction of a cabin on their lot. I was shocked to note that this cabin was to be something of a small skyscraper, taller than the large, mature trees in the area. I told the landowners that such a structure was unacceptable and urged them to revise the plan for something of lower profile that would not stick out like a sore thumb on Lake McDonald. There are several cabin existing at Kelly Camp but Park visitors driving Going-To-The-Sun Road across the lake rarely notice the buildings because they are low profile and tucked in among the trees.

Bighorn Sheep, Glacier National Park, Montana

I tried to deal with the landowners but they were adamant about building their cabin any way they wanted, so I utilized an authority rarely used, and with approval of my Regional Director and the Montana Congressional Delegation, condemned the property. I only know of this type of action happening twice in the Park's history.

There was one strange and humorous incident that happened in our land acquisition program. A Youth Conservation Corp was working in the Park to clean up some areas that had been overused or abused. The Park Service had recently purchased an inholding at Charlie Green Subdivision, located at the junction of the North Fork and Middle Fork Rivers in the southwest portion of the Park. The YCC group had the task of burning down the cabin and restoring the property to a natural condition. About a month later I was working late at the office one night and someone was banging on the back door. I went to let them in and found a young couple from California, who explained that they owned a cabin at Charlie Green Subdivision. They were traveling through the area and intended to spend the night at their cabin, but couldn't find it. My immediate thought was, Oh-oh, something has gone wrong with the YCC cleanup operation. This couple is from California and we are in for a big time lawsuit.

I explained to the couple what might have happened, but I was in for an even bigger surprise. The California couple said they were traveling through the area on their way home and planned to spend the night at their cabin, then in the morning they planned to stop at my office and determine if the National Park Service would be interested in purchasing their property. I could hardly believe our good fortune and after recovering my composure, I assured them that we would be happy to purchase their property. I bought their dinner, rented a room for them and scheduled a meeting in the morning to complete our land acquisition deal.

There is another side bit of humor attached to this story. Tom Esch, one of the teenagers in the YCC group was from Kalispell and he eventually became an attorney and for a time was Flathead County Attorney. I had a lot of fun through the years reminding him of the time he was involved in a case of arson in Glacier National Park.

At this same time, private landowners of property within National Parks and National Forests became alarmed over this aggressive land acquisition program. A fellow named Cushman, I think from Nevada, used the opportunity to organize the National Park Inholders Association, and a local chapter was formed in Glacier National Park.

Mel Ruder, owner and editor of the Pulitzer Prize winning Hungry Horse News visited every week to gather news about the Park. Mel told me that printing a photograph of a bear on the front page of his newspaper would make for a significant increase in circulation and bears provided a lot of stories. The almost mystic bear mauling incidents of 1967 were the source of a book called "The Night of the Grizzly" which was also made into a movie and still seen on television.

Bears that became habituated to human food from raiding campgrounds and handouts from motorists had to be relocated. This was not a good solution but the only other alternative was killing the animal. Bears establish their own territory, so when an alien bear is introduced into foreign territory it disrupts the territory of the existing occupants. I used to compare it to a dish of marbles. When you pluck a marble from the dish and move it to another location it disrupts all the other marbles.

We did give troublesome bears to zoos and Professor Chuck Jonkel at the University of Montana for research purposes, but that was a limited market. Mr. Jonkel was working on a repellent for bears, including pepper spray which is now standard equipment for backcountry hikers.

Glacier National Park had several fatal bear mauling incidents, which were caused by the bear management policies of years past. Bears were hanging out along roadsides begging for handouts from passing motorists, they were raiding food supplies from backcountry campers and feeding at exposed garbage dumps. Years ago Yellowstone National Park even had bleachers erected at the garbage dump to entertain Park visitors by watching bears eat the garbage. We developed an intensive bear management plan to correct these past mistakes and I involved every employee of the Park to develop the plan. After all, the maintenance employee who cleans campgrounds knows about bear incidents, trail crews working in the backcountry are aware of bear behavior, the Park naturalists who give campfire programs have a big part in the program by communicating with Park visitors, and of course the Park rangers are involved in closing trails, trapping bears and closing areas that are hazardous to the public because of something that attracts bears. So, every employee has a part in bear management and the development of a plan to minimize or eliminate bear incidents. This is one of those difficult park management objectives of leaving the Park unimpaired and also providing for the public use and enjoyment. It's a task of merging the wild features of a Park with unaccustomed visitors from the city in strange surroundings.

Avalanche Lake, Glacier National Park, Montana

I was attending a Superintendents' meeting in Denver and received a phone message from Glacier National Park to inform me that a fatal bear mauling had occurred at the Many Glacier campground, so a plane was chartered to fly back to the Park. Three girls from the University of Montana came to camp in Glacier. They entered the Park at the West Glacier entrance and the ranger at the entrance station clearly recalled their entry. One of the girls was very concerned about bears and the ranger went through the list of precautions they should take, like store food in their car well away from the campsite, don't wear cosmetics, don't camp if they were having a female period and so on.

The girls traveled through the Park, exited at St. Mary and reentered the Park again at Many Glacier. The ranger at that entrance station also remembers their entry because of their unusual concern about bears, and again the ranger went through the list of precautions for avoiding a bear encounter.

The girls set up camp in Many Glacier campground which was filled to capacity, prepared dinner, sat around the campfire and finally all three crowded into a small pup tent to sleep. In the early morning hours an adolescent male grizzly bear was investigating the area and was attracted to the pup tent because there was movement of the tent. Young grizzly bears are playful and curious so this bear apparently attacked the tent, ripped it open and discovered Pat Mahoney, dragged her out of the tent, killed her and ate part of the flesh. The other two girls had fled to their car but the commotion aroused other campers who contacted the ranger campground tender. Armed with a rifle he organized a search for Miss Mahoney and as daylight broke they found the body. The bear was later identified and disposed of. It was an eerie story because of the girls' unusual concern over bears, almost a premonition of what happened and certainly a tragic event.

I recall another bear incident that had a humorous ending. Two young men had hiked into Logging Lake on the west side of the Park, to camp at a remote site and do some fishing. They also slept in a pup tent set up near the shore of the lake. During the night a young, male grizzly bear was investigating their campsite and eventually sat down on top of the pup tent. The boys were sleeping nude in mummy bags. Now mummy bags can be a little difficult to get in and out of, especially in a collapsed pup tent with a grizzly bear sitting on top. Eventually, one of the boys managed to extract himself from the tent and ran into the ice cold water of Logging Lake with the bear running after him, but fortunately the bear stopped at the water's edge. While the bear was concentrating on the boy in the lake, the other camper managed to free himself from the tent and he also ran to the lake.

The bear now left the lakeshore and returned to the tent and began dragging contents of the tent up the hillside. The boys ran toward the tent to salvage shoes, clothes and cameras, but each time they approached their tent the bear chased them back into the lake. This went on for a couple of hours, when to their good fortune a ranger on horseback patrol just happened to be passing by. He had a rifle and scared the bear away so that the young men could salvage their possessions and retreat from the scene.

Another story about bears is this excerpt from my diary, October 23, 1974. J. Gordon Edwards, author of a book on hiking trails of Glacier National Park, was bushwhacking through brush and thimble berry in Many Glacier Valley when he encountered a sow grizzly bear, unaware that he had come between the sow and her two cubs. The bear charged him and his first instinct was to defend himself with an ice axe that he had attached to his belt. However, upon second thought he realized this would not be very effective. As the bear continued toward him, Mr. Edwards placed his left arm and hand in front of him, as if to ward off the attack. The bear bit his hand and maintained a grip, so Mr. Edwards looked at the bear face to face and talked in mellow tones, making remarks like, "Just be calm old girl, I'm not going to hurt your cubs, let's just calm down now."

After a few seconds the bear released Mr. Edwards hand and departed with her cubs. This incident illustrates two points. One, in most grizzly bear encounters the bear is not looking for trouble but just protecting the cubs or a food source, so hikers must keep this in mind. Don't get between a mother bear and her cubs. The second point is male grizzly bears are known to kill their own cubs but the females are wonderful, patient and protective parents.

Wolves were not transplanted in Glacier Park, but they probably drifted south from Canada and this is ranger Jerry DeSanto's report of his first encounter. Superintendent's daily log or diary from May 22, 1975. Report of a wolf sighting in the North Fork area of Glacier National Park by sub-district ranger Jerry DeSanto. "ULM grid coordinates are 5410.8 x 699.3. The weather was cloudy and about 50F. We had walked up through a meadow above the homestead about 30 minutes earlier and scared up two elk there. When we saw the wolf, we were retracing our steps to the southwest. We spotted the wolf about 100 feet from us in the open meadow. We were also in the open. He had his nose to the ground and did not see us until about 15 seconds after we saw him. When he saw us, he loped off into the woods. It was an unmistakable sighting."

The Garden Wall, Glacier National Park, Montana

Feb 5, 1979. Phoned National Park Service Director Bill Whalen to discuss personal plans. This was probably a follow up of my phone conversation with Director Whalen on June 30. A friend of mine named James Carrico was working in the Washington Office of the National Park Service, on a committee that made up lists of candidates for vacant positions throughout the National Park Service. Jim tipped me off that I was going to be offered the job of Superintendent of Great Smoky Mountain National Park. This is a challenging position in a high profile Park close to Washington DC. I would accept the position in a heart beat, but our plans are to retire in Montana and if I accepted the transfer, we would have to pay for our move back to Montana when I retired, within two or three years. Also, our daughter Pam, at an awkward time, would be forced to transfer schools, so considering those circumstances I told Jim that I would like to be deleted from this offer. The most unusual offer and decline of a transfer I had ever made - nothing on paper.

Aug. 16, 1979 Staff Meeting. Mr. Lon Garrison attended this staff meeting.   Lon has been working as a volunteer in the Park this summer. He was Assistant Superintendent of Glacier during the years of WWII. He served in the Washington Office, Regional Director at Philadelphia, Superintendent of Yellowstone, etc. He received his first job with the U.S. Forest Service in 1929 as a Forest Guard. His duty was to patrol the Alaska Railroad behind the trains to control fires started by burning coal sparks from the train. Mr. Garrison has worked for every Director of the National Park Service except Stephen Mather, the first Director.

Mr. Garrison said, "Mather was the first director, but Horace Albright, Assistant Director, was the one that got the House and Senate to agree on the Parks Bill (legislation that established the National Park Service as a new government agency to manage the National Parks)." Several National Parks had been established prior to this time with no coordinated management. There were different versions in the House and Senate. The bill was introduced in 1908, but not passed until 1916. Mather was in the backcountry of the Sierras at the time the bill was passed.

Sometimes it takes a long time between the inception of an idea until it comes to fruition. It was about the summer of 2005 that a transportation center was constructed near Apgar in Glacier National Park. Here are notes from a staff meeting on September 18, 1979 when we first discussed the idea. At the staff meeting today we discussed a possible expansion of the Park transportation system, which presently is used almost exclusively to move visitors from one hotel to another. We need a transportation system that would meet visitors at the railway stations, airport, stop at trailheads in the Park, etc. Mr. Don Hummel, owner of Glacier Park Inc. concession has shown some interest in this idea. The big problem is how to fund this system.

At this staff meeting a Development Concept Plan for the Apgar area was discussed, including the future location of a Visitor Center. The "T" intersection was considered to be a good location with minimal impact on Park ecology, but the possibility of a joint visitor center outside the Park, with the U.S. Forest Service is also under consideration. This is an interesting idea but I would be concerned about the complications of future funding for the facility, with appropriations coming from two different departments of the federal government. At some future date one agency may have adequate funding and the other agency may not. Then what happens? Also, if the visitor center is located within the Park, employees at the entrance station have a place to send visitors for information, because they don't have time for answering many questions. If the Visitor Center is located outside the Park it would not be helpful for the entrance station employees.

Mountain Goats, Glacier National Park, Montana

A five-mile section of U.S. Highway 2 cuts through the southern part of Glacier National Park. An interesting feature along this section of road is a goat lick, a mineral deposit that mountain goats need in their diet for their digestive system to function properly, especially when new grass emerges in the spring months of the year. Goats can frequently be seen on this steep cliff side and it is a popular viewpoint for visitors. Also at this location is a bridge on U.S. Highway 2 that crosses a steep ravine. I think it was in the winter of 1977 - 1978 that an avalanche came down the ravine, tore the bridge from its foundation and sent it to the bottom of the mountain like a giant toboggan. My diary of April 19, 1979 makes note of this event.

April 19, 1979 Meeting with Federal Highway Adm. on new bridge, at Goat Lick, on U.S. Hwy. 2. Old bridge had been torn out by an avalanche and carried to the bottom of the canyon.

July 2, 1979 Float trip down Middle Fork of Flathead River to examine the old Goat Lick bridge, which had been carried to bottom of canyon by an avalanche. We need to make a decision on what to do with the wreckage.

Regional Director Lynn Thompson appointed me as "State Coordinator" for the state of Montana. My job was to be the National Park Service representative and contact person for other federal and state agencies. I would report on events happening in the state that would be of interest to the National Park Service and also make periodic inspection of National Historic Sites and Landmarks within the state.

One of the more interesting events I covered as State Coordinator was the dedication of Grant Kohrs Ranch in Deer Lodge, Montana. From my diary Nov. 6 - 7, 1979. Travel to Grant Kohrs Ranch in Deer Lodge as part of State Coordinator job. When I was Assistant Regional Director in the Omaha, Nebraska office, from April 1970 to June 1972, we were negotiating for the purchase of Grant Kohrs Ranch as a National Park area to represent the western ranching scene of the 19th century. The property is a perfect example of the western ranch of that era and this property in particular is an amazing time capsule. The ranch grazed cattle on the open range throughout most of Montana and even into parts of Wyoming.

Mr. Kohrs had passed away, their only son died of appendicitis rupture, the only daughter had left home for points unknown. Mrs. Kohrs lived at the ranch during summer months and spent the winters in Helena. One year she was unable to return to the ranch and her nephew, I think, who lived next door, locked all doors to the house and allowed nothing to be removed. The house was preserved as a perfect time capsule, the furniture, pictures and clocks on the walls, dishes and cooking utensils in the kitchen, clothes in the dresser drawers and everything left intact from the day Mrs. Kohrs left the house.

It was a stroke of rare good fortune that this unique ranch could be acquired for inclusion in the National Park system. This ranch was the setting for Michener's book "Centennial", but in the story he transferred the scene to the state of Colorado. The Kohrs family was the principle characters of the book. I was transferred from the Regional Office in Omaha to State Director of the National Parks in Utah with my office in the Federal Building in Salt Lake City. February 1, 1974 I was transferred to Glacier National Park as Superintendent and shortly after arriving in Montana, I had the pleasure of attending the dedication of the Grant Kohrs ranch as a unit of the National Park System, so I have had a particular interest in this place.

Superintendent's log Nov. 5, 1979. Jim Bose, former owner of business near Lake McDonald Lodge moved from property. He has been a problem to the Park for a long time and happy for his departure. In the November 13 staff minutes I noted that "three years ago the NPS made an agreement with Chairman Yates (U.S. House of Representatives) that we would dispose of the structures when an inholding was acquired." The Park Service purchased this property, the transaction is now complete and the land will be restored to a natural condition.

Several movies have been filmed in Glacier Park and perhaps the most famous one was Heaven's Gate directed by Michael Cimino, winner of an Academy Award the previous year. Mr. Cimino came to our home in the Park one weekend with a proposal to film a movie in the Two Medicine area. He had just completed a movie called the Deer Hunter, which had several nominations for the forthcoming Academy Award banquet. Michael told me that the movie would be about the Johnson County War, a conflict that took place between cattle ranchers and sheep ranchers near Buffalo, Wyoming. As it happened, my parents had homesteaded on a small sheep ranch just a few miles east of Buffalo so this story was of considerable interest to me.

Mr. Cimino proposed to erect a fairly sizeable movie set near the shore of Two Medicine Lake. I was very much concerned with the environmental impact this would have on native vegetation. The filming would have virtually no disruption to visitor use because it was scheduled to be completed by the end of May, before the visitor season began. The idea of filming a movie in the Park was intriguing because the movie story was an actual historic event and most of all, it would provide the public who couldn't travel to Montana, with a good view of Glacier National Park. I recruited other members of my staff to work out details of a contract that would protect the natural resources of the Park and not disrupt visitor use.

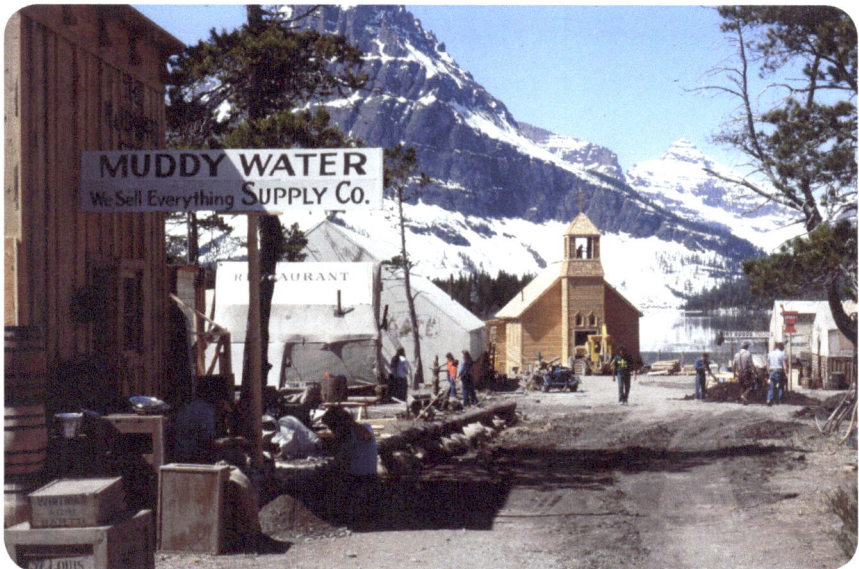

Heaven's Gate Movie Set, Two Medicine Lake, Glacier N. P.

There was considerable risk in granting such a permit. It was my experience in working with movie people that they had a big ego, convinced that everyone would be thrilled to work with the glamorous movie people, and most of them didn't have the vaguest idea what a National Park was all about.

As the movie production progressed, Mr. Cimino strayed from the original storyline and eventually there was no connection to the Johnson County War. He became more and more impressed with himself and his achievement as a Best Director nominee for an Academy Award. He began adding scenes to the movie and spending huge amounts of investors' money, many times over budget. The investors were getting nervous and hired a tall businessman of oriental ancestry to monitor Mr. Cimino. This gentleman took me aside one day and told me, "If Michael Cimino wins the Academy Award there is going to be hell to pay, from then on he's going to think that he is untouchable.

His prophecy came true. The movie was now four hours long, the people financing it were forced into bankruptcy and the movie became notorious in Hollywood for its colossal failure. My patience with Mr. Cimino had reached the limit and it came to a conclusion when he slaughtered a cow in the Park, an attraction for grizzly bears, and the contract time limit was exceeded by a couple weeks. I cancelled the contract and instructed Mr. Cimino and company to be out of the Park within one week.

I caught a lot of guff for awhile, mostly from the Kalispell business community because this production was pumping a lot of money into the town and a lot of people were working as extras and laborers. However, to his credit, Mr. Cimino did an excellent job of cleaning up the site, but he did take a few parting shots at me.

If I had my life to live over again, I would again choose a career with the National Park Service in a heartbeat. That is not to say that everything was always peaches and cream, but that is true of any career choice. I recall a survey in years past in which the public was asked, what is your favorite government agency. The National Park Service came out on top, which surprised me because we are a small agency and I didn't think that many people were aware of us.

It's necessary to differentiate between all National Parks collectively and the National Park Service as a government agency. The agency is not all that distinctive from any other government agency. Maybe a little higher on the totem pole because so many of the employees are very dedicated, with an almost cult like commitment to the mission of the agency.   On the other hand, except for the numerous National Park Service memorials and monuments around Washington DC, I will make a guess that most employees of the National Park Service in Washington or any of the several Regional Offices have never worked in a National Park, and in fact some may never have even visited a National Park.

Unfortunately, the power base of the agency is in Washington DC and the Regional Offices. This is where budgets are finalized, where final priorities are decided and where important decisions are made. Consequently, the needs of Parks tend to be a lower priority than the needs of these higher offices. Also, Regional Directors and their staff will eventually meddle more and more into decisions the Park Superintendent and their staff should be making. This is why I maintain that when talking about the National Park Service, I am referring to the Parks themselves, not the government agency called the National Park Service.   We must maintain a constant vigil to protect the National Parks, sometimes from the agency that administers them.

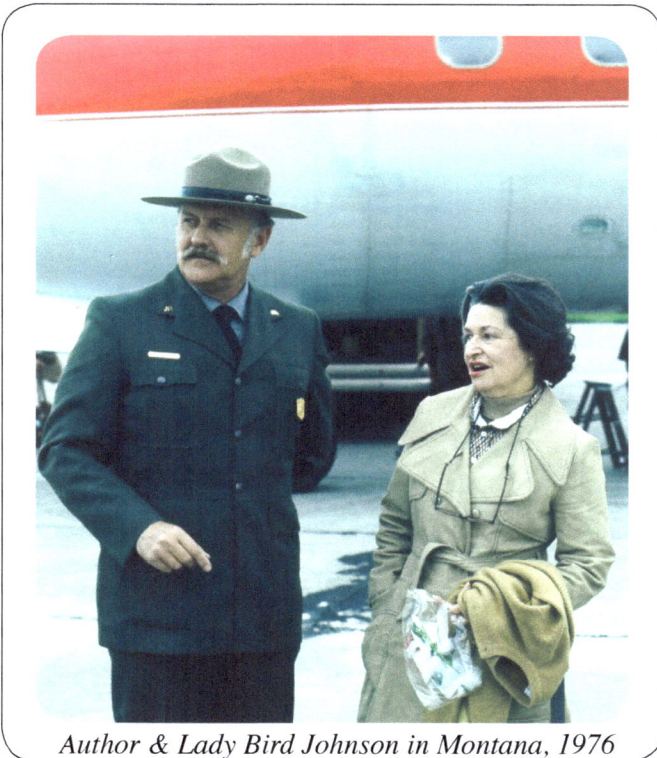

Author & Lady Bird Johnson in Montana, 1976